PRIMITIVES
Our American Heritage

by

Kathryn M. McNerney

COLLECTOR BOOKS
A Division of Schroeder Publishing Co., Inc.
P.O. BOX 3009 • PADUCAH, KENTUCKY 42001

JACKET COLOR ILLUSTRATIONS

Front:	*Top Row Left to Right*	
	SLEIGHBELLS, burnished brass, 23 etched and numbered graduated sizes, open center bell, original leather strap . . .	$ 375.00
	GRAIN SORTER (SIEVE), all original	45.00
	ROPE BED WRENCH, 18th century	100.00
	Lower Left to Right	
	IRON KETTLE, sliding top	175.00
	WAGON TOOL BOX, all original, maker's name each end in ornamental iron	140.00
	HAND CORNSHELLER c: 1870	55.00
	BLUEBILL DECOY, original, handcarved, signed	150.00
Back:	*Top Row Left to Right*	
	OXEN TRAINER YOKE, all original, handcut	145.00
	CURD BREAKER, cheese, could have been used also as a food chopper, blacksmith signed, early	125.00
	FIELD BULL BELL, brass, metal worn shorter one side from swinging, leather strap	100.00
	Below Left to Right	
	GRAINS (RICE) MORTAR & PESTLE, 18th century, handfashioned from 1 block of hickory wood, forged iron band, hanging ring	250.00
	LINEN SMOOTHER, rounded corrugations, 1 pc. wood handcut	115.00
	CHAMBERSTICK, brass and copper, thumblift	140.00
	MEASURE, papier mache'	50.00
	SEALING WAX CROCKS	30.00

Additional copies of this book may be ordered from:

COLLECTOR BOOKS
P.O. Box 3009
Paducah, Kentucky 42001

@ $8.95 Add $1.00 for postage and handling.

Dealers and clubs should write for quantity discounts.

PRIMITIVES . . . OUR AMERICAN HERITAGE

and how they changed and progressed from the frontiers into the 1890s

DEDICATION

For the fifth Kathryn

CONTENTS

APPRECIATION

Shops may display a sign calling antiquing a disease . . . I disagree . . . exposure can become a way of life and in choosing a field personally most challenging for a collection the Primitives are sort of like olives . . . you do . . . or you don't . . . and I do!

Faced with trying to identify a difficult piece on which I had grossly overbid at a country auction in the exciting competition of my "first" such purchase (not my "last" although I've grown more wary) I was drawn deeper and deeper into the fabulous World of Primitives, recklessly but happily adventuring into the maze of extended research, encouraged by others already involved.

And for still more assistance from generously cooperative friends I am grateful to:

Mr. John L. M. Taylor, Atlanta, Georgia for much of the photography; to

Mr. L.E. Skelton, Manager of the Antebellum Plantation, Stone Mountain Park, Georgia, who not only welcomed us but himself selected appropriate artifacts for pictures, meanwhile offering regional information, (Plantation designated); to
Mr. and Mrs. Burwick Downs, Cadiz, Kentucky, Mr. and Mrs. Wayne Abercrombie, East Peoria, Illinois, and Mrs. Jill Wasson, Straughn, Indiana, their items noted; and to an enthusiastic Dealer who prefers anonymity.

All other collectibles were mine as this book was being written.

My deep appreciation embraces my husband Tom and my Sis Dotty Fellows, Avondale Estates, Georgia . . . they my patient and constant Listeners!

And as staunchly as time itself endures so does my gratitude continue for the endless pages I have been and may ever be able to read of undistinguishable American History and its Primitives; for the stories and sayings carefully related to me by innumerable kindly folks native to areas still reflecting a way, a phrase, or a legend of its past.

Hopefully, may I share with you this fun and fascination.

BACKGROUND

"Cripes! Nuthin' else t' do . . . y' jist had t' rig up suthin' t' git by a't'all."

Thus an American Settler straining t' make out on a raw homestead torn from the wilderness stretching in several directions from our eastern seacoast towns might best have described the existence of those treasures we now seek and preserve . . . the PRIMITIVES.

This same man (flushed with reluctant pride tho grinning hugely) would have awkwardly shrugged our admiration of his manual efforts; but he could never have readily understood our dismay at his endless brutally hard work sustained only by desperate bravery, scarred horny hands, and his lonely self-reliance such a "deal-uv-a-ways frum his root-kin".

For to him . . . primitives were necessities.

And to us . . . primitives are heritage.

All the variable traits and circumstances of his forebears existing under precarious liberties had finally erupted into the ambitious American Pioneer . . . eager to own . . . determined to hold onto!

When the limited supplies he'd "brung along played out" he made others to his urgencies according to his own notions and abilities; shelter, clothing, housekeeping, implements to challenge and subdue the soil, and implements to build further and maintain, using materials in and on and over the ground and in the waters, all herein considered frontier tools for survival.

But above all, "when lackin' Meetin' House Preachin' " he himself kept Faith, one hand on the axe or the plow, one hand on his dogeared Bible, and his gun always close at his side.

So 'twas . . . the man made the tools, the tools sustained the man. To speak of one is to recall the other, like which came first, the chicken or the egg . . . and the strongest of each weathered through.

Clear into the last century with the western plains and mountains almost undisturbed until after 1865 dense forests bowed steadily to the bite of iron. Indians taught the first pioneers differences between woods and their best usages and that trees more easily cut in February when the sap is still fairly dormant dried faster in March winds. Thomas Jefferson wrote a friend in the late 1700s that almost 6,000 trees had to be cut to claim land for an average farm in Pennsylvania and New York.

Where a cluster of cabins was raised, as the first mark of respectability toward becoming an outpost, a Minister and a Farrier (a blacksmith who additionally shod animals) were urged to settle, sometimes with the inducement of free lands. Quickly followed by the itinerant tinner these introduced a steady refinement and uniformity of design into their practical wares.

And each craftsman expressed his cleverness in lighter ways, being in great demand for "weddin' presunts", for some means of making "jis'-one-right-hard-pull easier", this last where always before had been too few tools for too many tasks.

Wherever an object is called one thing when you are positive it is another, then the question should be open for further exploration rather than a heated argument. For instance, your ancestor may have used a certain piece he'd made for a job utterly unlike that for which a neighbor applied something almost identical, one probably having derived the idea from the other in the first place. Resultant individual touches would then have led to the one-of-a-kinds that today can be so frustrating to identify even though we discover look-alikes and similars of the same period. But whichever puzzler resists specific historical conclusion can be fun to calk'late since Primitives and their kin rank high among the truly intriguing "Conjecturables".

Nor can we dismiss all Primitives as "crudities". They are eloquent in homey, honest ways. Slowly they achieved real or doubtful comforts. As the years droned on with his homestead rights becoming more secure the Settler roused to an impatient awareness that beyond the lovely natural vistas he was beginning to have time to really SEE he yearned to attain beauty in something he himself could at least try to make.

This he "thought on't fer quite a spell". "I-doggities . . . he would!" Gradually the aches of the days' labors were forgotten in the evenings' thrills of manipulating his small tools for pleasure as well as practicality.

His excitement transcended even the choking fumes of the bear fat in the grease lamps and his having to squint and shift at fireside. May we notice with understanding a pathetically-tender carving on a cradle satin-smoothed, the anxious lines of a wistful toy, such proudly-curving arms on a chair that crookedly rocks, or soft berry-dye shadings that fed only the eye . . . and the heart.

And the outposts grew into settlements . . . and the settlements grew into towns.

Next started a slow but firm transition from early pioneer living into the 1800s. Wondrous cookstoves dispensed with redcheeked bending over kettles bubbling at the open hearth or blistered fingers lifting a steaming pot off the trammel hook using the edge of an apron for protection; pottery and thick china were carried backpack along with the usual wooden and tinware even to remote areas by walking peddlers, then in saddlepacks slung over the backs of horses or mules, finally in carts and wagons; "an' idle-purty-pieces traded-fer er bought by th' menfolks jis' t' be a'givin' made th' cabins a mite cheerfuller". After 1859 kerosene generally replaced fishoils, grease, candles, and whale oil, surface petroleum distilled until commercial drilling was successful.

From those faraway yesterdays the actual savage hardships could never be today's memories; how fortunate indeed we do have revealing material echoes of the homesteaders' lives.

Despite colors dimmed and edges frayed and dulled in the patina of the ages they will forever be footsteps forward . . . doggedly . . . rambunctiously . . . thankfully . . . patiently . . . hewn by the American Settler.

And to hold in our hands the Primitives he made is to purely touch the past.

"ca." for "CIRCA"

Everyone without a heavy purse who disembarked onto American shores in the earliest and continuing days of colonization had to eke out a living somehow . . . and tall or short, fat or thin, strong or weak, timid or brave . . . those with a dream hacked it out from the wilderness.

Primitives, then, could represent the average American, average considered to be the inherent or inherited capabilities that surfaced when his survival depended upon his own ingenuity regardless of his talents or lack of them . . . he simply did the best he could with the tools and circumstances at hand . . . trying to recall how such was put together in the "Old Country" and adjusting it in a commonsense down-to-earth-approach to his immediate needs . . . and making it to "hold up".

The emergence of those efforts are the objects our forebears with dirt under their fingernails left for us to enjoy and cherish.

The frontiers were many years in developing . . . formation and use of the Primitives kept pace. Determining precise dates is for me impractical and well nigh impossible unless I know the family where something was "handed down". At best I CAN use the word "Circa" meaning "about". It is possible, however, to approximate from style and appearance. Good designs in tools and furniture, for instance, changed very slowly and in small degree, many forms in use today almost the same as two hundred years ago. Mortise and tenon joints were familiar to ancient Greeks while dovetailing was used by the early Egyptians.

Quantity production set in after 1865 to destroy much individual Americana as Victorians demanded a whole new "look"; fancier and endless intricate touches combined with orders for prompt delivery caused many of the beautifully-plain lines and handcrafting to disappear.

So as the Settler did when faced with such a variable task I will simply calk'late to do my best in supplying approximate dates to the research information at hand . . . and use "ca." for "CIRCA".

ON THE LAND

Soon after cabins began to appear the GRIST MILL, a vital part of the homesteader's life, was built at the nearest stream having a good flow. This granite BUHRSTONE was half of a pair that between them ground flour and meal, revolving under waterpower channeled into a millrace canal for current, thence over huge waterwheels, activating a gear train that turned the many sized stones comprising the unit. When the stones became heavily worn a blacksmith might forge an iron band around the uneven edge for smoother grinding.

The smithy-made PICKS dressed (sharpened and cleaned) the millstones.

(An elderly farmer seeing me buy the stone said it so reminded him of his great-uncle's mill he could almost smell the crushed grain.)

This peck GRAIN MEASURE with wrapped wooden topband, a little bigger than a Toll Measure, has the owner's name carved in the bottom. ca: 1880s.

"It shur tuk awhile t' shell th' two bushels a'corn" needed to fill one of these earliest-made double-woven cotton GRAIN BAGS for milled and unmilled grains, if you had to rub one hard yellow ear " 'gainst t'other" prior to handcranked home shellers. Toted over a shoulder or slung animal-back the filled sacks were carried to the grist mill to be cracked or ground into meal, the miller keeping about one-fourth of the grain as payment. Handy for tough topclothes and scratchy underwear several bags handstitched together became mattress kivers for soaked, dried, and cut-up rustly cornshucks; they might even provide the breathtaking luxury of a curtain! Earlier sacks were woven by th' missus. ca.: 1880s.

Tediously carrying water from a stream the settler built his WELL over a spring as quickly as possible. On a wooden framework a length of rough log with an iron handle burned through hauled up wooden buckets tied to a rope which wrapped around the windlass as it turned. From the 1840s this well has a later replacement metal bucket with an added wellcover and roof. Plantation.

A large leather-belt-driven wooden PULLEY (WHEEL), powered by water from the millstream, was in use at a Henry County, Tennessee, Grist Mill during the 1880s.

A shorter WELL WHEEL remained with three WELL HOOKS at an early 1800s cabin site; a rotting wooden bucket lay near the Well's 3-board top frame insecure on a crumbling clay-stuck fieldstone wall. The forged GRAPPLING HOOKS, iron bars heated and bent to form the eyes could retrieve waterbuckets that slipped off the rope and containers of food lost when lowered into the water for cooling; they could double as meatholders in fireplace cookery.

A windmill pumped water. It was a complicated machine for the 1800s, such new implements gathering momentum in that century from the ideas and inventive efforts of the pioneers in the 1700s to reach beyond their basic tools. As wind velocity increased the top mechanism actuated by the 9 lb. factory-marked iron CHICKEN WINDMILL WEIGHT caused the wind control rudder (arm) to turn in either direction, moving the blades out of the path of the wind to slow down the windmill, at times almost to a stop. This action was taken to protect the plunger rod from damage . . . from running wild. The normal turning of the blades caused the pump below to pull up the water.

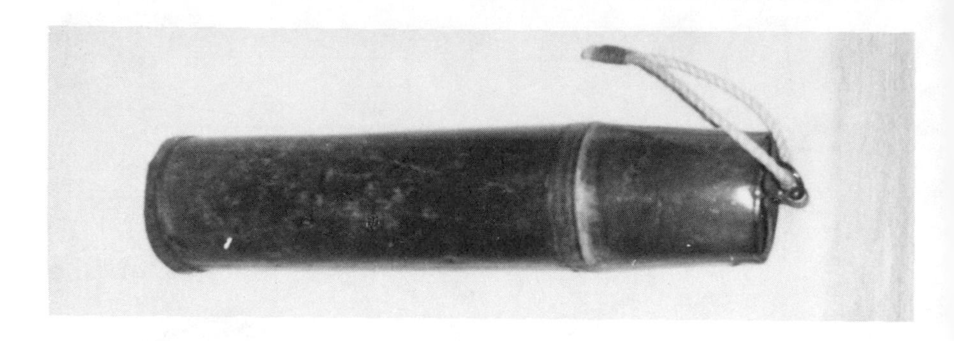

A step from the earlier open wells, this iron WELL BUCKET or tube in the latter 1800s was dropped into a driven well. As it sank into the well a base inside leather flap opened to allow the water to fill the tube. As it was lifted out of the well the weight of the water in the tube caused the leather valve to close so no water could escape. At the surface the long iron Bucket could be tipped to pour into piggins or similar containers.

"Heavy-as-all-git-out" a smithy-made LOG DRAG used by three generations during the 1800s. Chains fastened at the top, sharp corners bit into an axe-felled tree, and the whole harnessed to oxen was snaked from the forest, preferably while enough snow was still left on the ground to make dragging easier.

A BARKING SPUD removed rough bark from felled trees, the iron band an old and usual style of the smithy. ca: 1850.

The 3 ft. long lightly used hickory HITTING MAUL split rails by striking the IRON WEDGE. ca: 1870-80.

A COMMANDER is a good example of the same object for several uses. Its handcut hickory with debarked sappling handle helped raise a Tennessee cabin, swung between the legs to drive home a shaped log into a mortise and tenon joint. Not marring the logs the faces of the Commander were mashed. Once the shelters were built it became in usage a HITTING BEETLE swung over the shoulder as an axe, hitting the top of an iron wedge driving the wedge into the timbers to split off fence rails, this last causing heavy shallow splinters on both striking surfaces. ca: 1860.

Oak Gluts were often used as wedges instead of iron.

Around the 1840s a SHAPING AXE with the straighter handle typical of that period shaped and squared the ends of logs intended for posts. Plantation.

Among the earliest of the frontier tools a T-BAR AUGER with the primitive straight handle was used to bore holes to fit wood pins when framing cabins. The SPIRAL AUGER made larger holes in heavier timbers as ships' planks, for instance. Its handle indicates after 1850.

The very early CARPENTER'S MALLET on its original handle drove in wooden pins (treenails or trunnels). (A PIN and a PEG are used interchangeably; when the Pin is pointed it is generally called Peg; both fastened or held together, or plugged a hole as in a cask; became wall holders for clothing, lanterns, light chairs, all sorts of things.)

A BURL (wart, canker knot usable from ash and maple trees with some walnut applicable in furniture inlay) STONECUTTER'S MAUL from c: 1790 that did not shatter in consistently striking an iron wedge. With the firming slash-pegged handle end through its base, the worn side indicates the hitting habit of one owner.

Typical of an even earlier date is this 1840s BEEHIVE homemade from a hollow beegum tree. Sticks wedged in crosswise supported wax honeycombs. With a shelter board across the top, sitting flat on another board, the whole was placed on stones or planks away from dampness. Five sawtooth cuts gave easy access. Horseshoes were later added for better handling.

Dependent on the weather, nearness of flowers, and the size of their swarm the busily buzzing honeybees could herein deposit up to forty pounds. After rags were burned to smoke out the agitated occupants the sticky mass was periodically removed by scooping and digging with long handcut wooden paddles and spoons. "Th' tarnal stuff ran all over a'body and down the outside of the Hive where it had to be scraped off. But it wuz shur mighty tasty fer sweet'nin' on hoecakes er soppin' up with biskits".

Some fellers robbed wild bees of honey stashed in holler trees in the woods being wary of a bearcritter on the same errand. Plantation.

A pre-1850 copper SUGAR SKIMMER found in Louisiana has square nail holes punched in its folded-edge ladle, allowing syrup to drop back into a huge kettle as it skimmed off the greenish scum bubbling to the top of the crushed cane during its first cooking stage -Grande'.

A Georgia Sea Islands smithy made this big SUGAR CLEAVER on its thick wooden base around the mid-1800s. Customarily kept on the sugarchest in the dining room it was ready for use in hacking off pieces of crystallized teasugar for the sugarbowl. Flanked by large teapots, sugarbowls grew ever-larger, sometimes several on one table keeping up with the family's affluence. (Large creamers were considered in poor taste since almost every family kept a cow and cream was ordinary.) was ordinary.)

During this period sugar for domestic use was shipped in cones about 18" high and a foot around wrapped for protection in indigo-blue-treated paper, this latter doubly important to the homemaker because she could soak the paper and reuse the dyes.

While not perfect the SUGAR NIPPERS did provide a lot of sugar particles and for many years were the only cutters folks had. Uncrystallized sugar pounded and ground for use in kitchens was called "basin sugar".

Made and used by Moravians in Massachusetts more than a century ago is this rather large tinned BUCKET in which the noonday meal was carried to a field worker. The tightly fitted Lid has a white porcelain knob. (Moravians were a religous sect who emigrated to America from Bohemia.) (Abercrombie).

A woodpegged GRAPE PRESS handcrafted during the latter 1800s. Grapes placed in the nailed-on tin center reservoir were pressed down firmly with the square movable plunger and the juices flowed out the round tin spigot at center front base into a bucket set below.

Such 1800s man-pushed mule-pulled SCOOTER PLOWS were used for many years in the southern cotton and corn fields for choppin' (weeding). It "stirred up th' groun' a mite" rather than clod the soil. These crops grow shallow and could be easily uprooted if too closely disturbed by the wider heavier-bladed breaking plows. The Scooter's narrow blade, smithy-repaired, (and top left handgrip gone) was attached by the HEELBOLT upper right. This tool endured to mechanization and can still be seen on remote patches. Plantation.

Named for a type of bird residue imported from South America a GUANO DISTRIBUTOR ("GUANER" in Alabama) was long ago used in cotton and corn fields man-pushed, mule-pulled. Also called a "KNOCKER" in Georgia, its wheel, two wooden slabs bolted together, knocked loudly against the iron release valve as it turned, causing a set amount of fertilizer to drop from the box down a crudely bent tin trough into the ground.

Both the small hickory SINGLETREE and the handcut pair of dogwood MULE HAMES with forged iron rings are proper size in harnessing a mule for this job.

A handcarved ca: 1820 MAPLE SUGAR MOLD of New England; after the cooked syrup poured in had hardened that wood best released the chunks. Note separate heart center designs.

WHETSTONE CARRIERS from the early 1800s are of thinly cut light wood (sometimes of easily carved animals' horns.) Worn even thinner a few wormholes increase their primitive good looks. Binder twine passed through eyes on the hump side fastened them to flat pieces of wood tucked behind the workers' belts. So carried to the fields they were pushed into the ground to hold water for cooling the Whetstones during the hand-sharpening of the big scythes and sickles . . . or held vinegar for cleansing the Stones.

This GRAIN FLAIL is a 4 ft. pole attached with leather thongs to a shorter, heavier hickory FLAIL having an iron swivel ball top. The pole held on the shoulder with the Flail hanging down the back was brought forward and down smartly with a practiced blow "just right" on grain already spread out to dry on the barn floor, the action of the Flail separating seeds from the chaff. ca: 1800s.

The wooden FIELD PEAS PLANTER has traces of original red paint, a metal tip and handle, and operated on the principle of the more universally used hand cornplanter a hundred years ago. When pushed by the iron handle into plowed ground the point pressure tripped back the plunger releasing the seed peas into the earth from a control slot thus opened in the base of the side tin container.

Two very old FIELD KNIVES were for handcutting corn while at right is an early SUGARCANE CUTTER. A smithy attached 2-piece wooden handles to the iron with forgemade rivets.

As far back as the early 1600s this chant of the workers describes their planting corn:

"One for the blackbird
One for the crow
One for the cutworm
And one to grow."

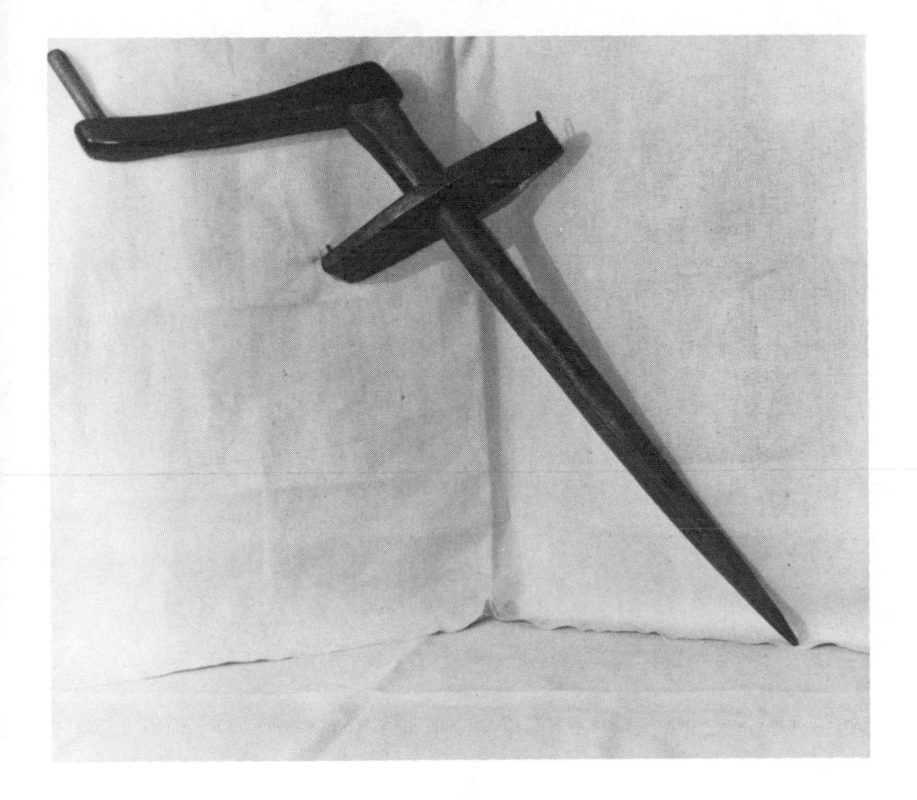

A century old 4-piece cherrywood STALK TYER has a bentwire nail in either end of the movable plateau below the turning handle. Upright with the point pushed into the ground in a harvest field, sheaves of grain or cornstalks were piled round in a circle; binder twine wrapped around the nails unwound to bind stalks together as the handle was turned. The tool was then lifted out of the center of the grain and the "shock" stood fairly upright on its own. Straw and hay were twisted into rope on a twiner if regular binder twine was not available.

An effectively crude COTTON INGIN (later shortened to GIN) gripped its splintery base with square nails in the mid-1800s. Turned in reverse the handles forced or pinched out the seeds which fell into the lower box. The ginned cotton was then lifted off by hand, this jerky-ginning the ancient principle of pinching out seeds. The contraption set on a plank table in a shed or under a tree on sweltering days had the dual purpose of stripping field peas from their pods. The iron COTTON BALE HOOK left is earliest, the right Hook unusual with double prongs, both forged. The later factory HOOK below is more often found.

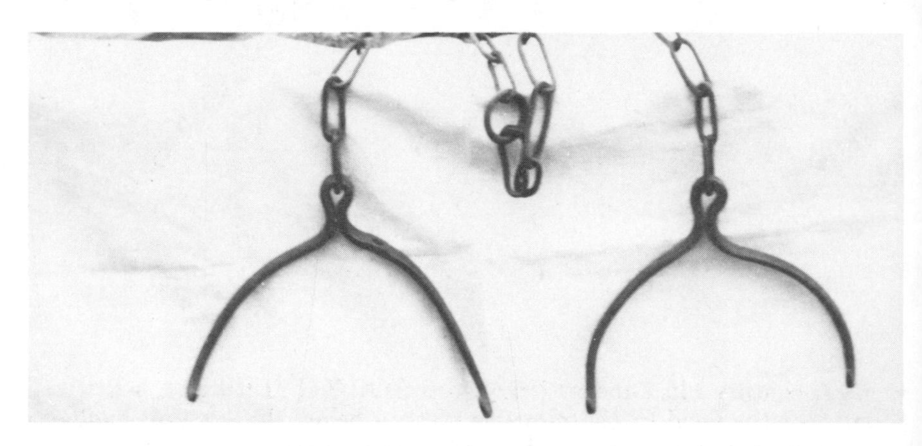

A pair of DOUBLE COTTON BALE HOOKS and CHAIN from Charleston, South Carolina in the 1700s is unusual. Four curved prongs grasped two bales and center rings attached to a lift raised them. Along with the typically-shaped chains, each double hook section was heated, curved, and bent from a single iron bar, revealing the careful skill of the blacksmith.

A steel FOX TRAP operated on much the same principle as the larger bear trap, description following.

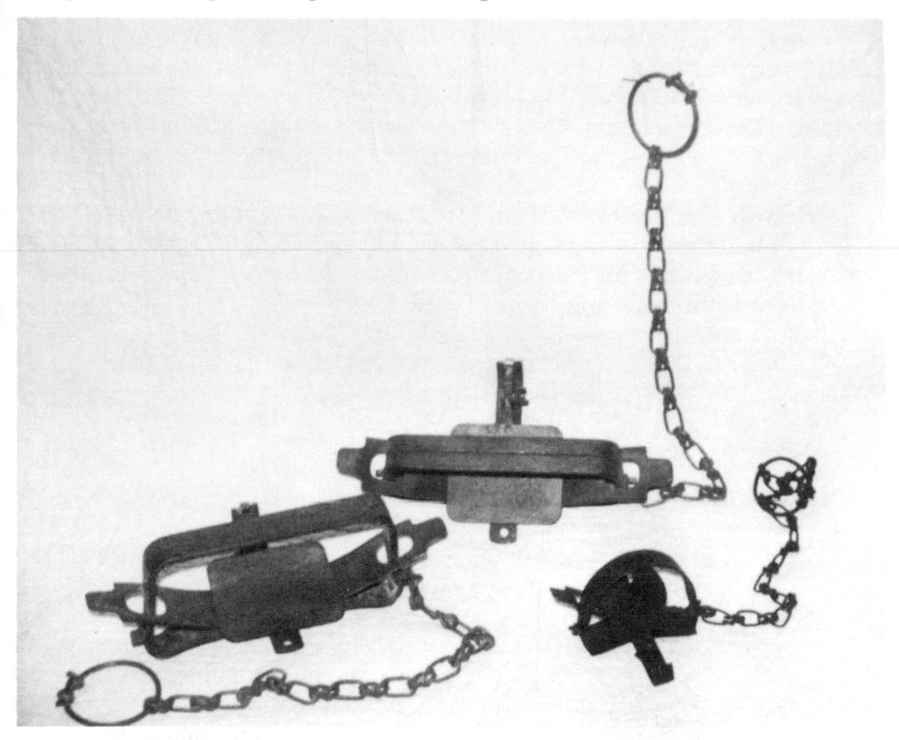

The Fox and the smaller size LEGHOLD ANIMAL TRAPS were judged by frontiersmen as the least dangerous way of trapping.

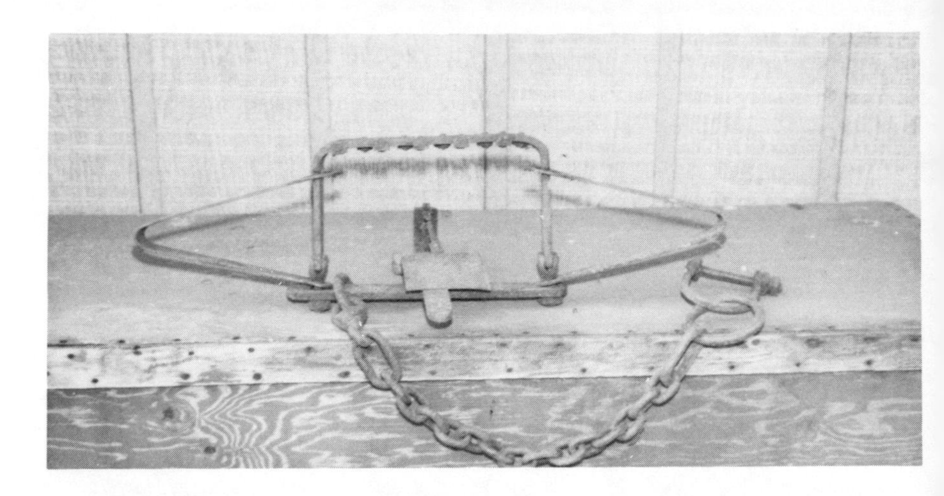

For BEAR TRAPS a sapling or suitable fallen tree branch could be used to open the jaws on their strong iron springs against hundreds of pressure pounds, risky to do by hand and taking extraordinary strength.

Held by chains hooked around a huge stone or tree, baits of meat or fish hung high or placed strategically low, with the inside deeply jagged teeth edges held open by the side bars, when a foot stepped onto the trip pan the small holding lever triggered the snapping shut of the jaws into the animals's leg; properly anchored the trap could not be dragged away.

However harsh the realism, it was one way a hungry homesteader could obtain meat for food, grease for injuries and lighting and furs for warmth and rugs, or trading for other goods . . . and eliminate predators from depleting his domestic livestock.

A 5-pound TURPENTINE ADZ regionally used well over a hundred years ago was blacksmith made for slashing turpentine pines to determine harvesting dates; its type of thick iron blade, wide iron band and round oak grip with one side worn flat could be one-of-a-kind.

A hollowed-out log in a smokehouse filled one side, set on end beams off a hard-packed dirt floor. Pork, easily cured and stored, was stacked in this SALT BIN a layer at a time with salt between, butchering done at the first cold snap as it is still done on many farms over the country. When cured, the bacon, shoulders, and hams taken from the Bin were wiped clean and sprinkled with borax to discourage an invasion of "skippers" (skipping insects). Plantation.

According to the owner's carefully guarded secret recipe for curing meats, herbs and peppers from his own gardens, dried and ground or pulverized, were combined with molasses to heavily coat the pork. Precious East Indian spices difficult to obtain were doled out daily from their individual tins nested in a locked box. For additional safety a Planter might lock the Spice Box in a chest in his bedroom.

The center TURPENTINE SPADE originally had a long branch handle; used to scrape off rosin dripping onto the tree's bark at various heights during slashing and harvesting. The right SCRAPER could gouge deeper than the Spade. The heavy forged LADLE at left is one piece of iron ingeniously shaped, twisted, and turned to form bowl and handle. ca.: 1880-1890 regional tools.

Revenooers wouldn't mistake these rare mallet-end MALT STICKS from a moonshine still over th' ridge. Their handcut whitely bleached wood proclaims the potency of the hot mash; and the reckless worms who burrowed into the handles and stirring knobs simply didn't have a "ghost uv a chanc't" in that brew. Around 1870.

In the late 1800s a blacksmith made-do from separates a 4 lb. TURPENTINE SLASHER, inserting the handle of a sharp lower edge factory tool into a split hardwood branch, anchoring it with a salvaged band and rivets, wedging the wood end into a massive iron round taken from something else. This practice termed "married off" or "marriage" is sometimes used for plain fakery or unintentional misrepresentation. Where this has occurred a very long time ago an object may now be accepted as genuine but this Slasher was openly put together and the owner said so. The Slasher grooved the regional pine allowing resin to drip into a bucket hung underneath.

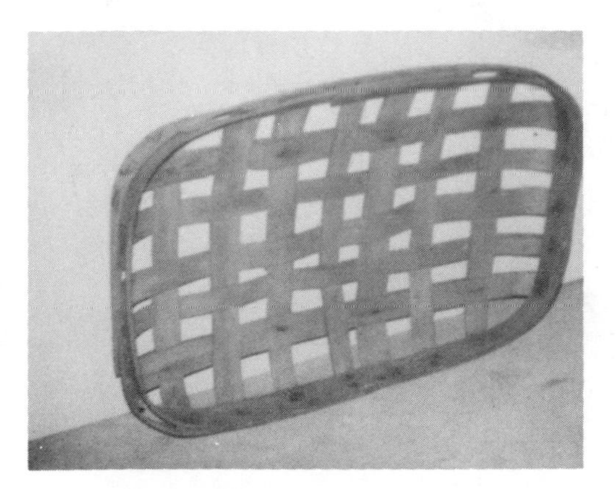

A large shallow TOBACCO WAREHOUSE BASKET wherein a farmer placed his "hands" of cured and stripped tobacco; the Basket numbered and set on the warehouse floor was ready for inspection until its contents were auctioned off to the highest bidder. Such Baskets have been used for more than a hundred years, still evident in some areas.

A TOBACCO HILLER Kentucky-used more than a hundred years ago. When the field was ready this man-pushed mule-pulled tool with its double-blade irons and uncommon WOODEN ROLLER "hilled" the ground for pegging (setting in) the young tobacco plants (much as sweet potatoes are now grown). (Downs).

Fieldcut TOBACCO PLANTS tied with twine to natural branch poles are hung for drying and leaf-stripping in an 1840s SHED of hand-hewn timbers. Plantation.

A stamped out oily brass MARKER under pressure imprinted STAG and a STAG'S HEAD on moistened processed tobacco, the lines shaping the cutting sizes although a customer could buy as little as 5¢ worth, a good sized piece. The broken bit of dried PLUG has a maker's TIN TAG, these now popular collectibles. A natural applewood knuckle TOBACCO PEG was to poke holes for field planting seedlings earlier sprouted from seeds under the same kind of cloth covered frames seen today. SLICERS (Cutters or Knives) were to manually harvest the matured plants, both this and the peggin' hard stoopwork (now mechanized). It would be unusual to find two Slicers exactly alike. Of similar design they were made to order or to the smithy's own ideas when he had a little spare time. c: 1890s.

Both barrel OPENERS were made in Virginia about 1850, the wooden with a metal tip and the iron with a hammer hump and a nail puller end.

Regionally a small patch of tobacco was grown at cabins much as it is today on far away places . . . the crop being cured, stripped, and twisted to the planter's taste.

At left a smithy-fashioned STORE TOBACCO CUTTER of iron on a thick block of wood cut plugs from a large pressed slab of tobacco, pressing the sharp edge with the handle. The CUTTER at right has a turned maple handle and was found in a Tobacconist's Shop. Both latter 1800s.

Kentucky Colonel was a popular brand as marked on the wooden SHIPPING BOX for cut plugs. ca: 1890s.

Fraternal Societies, known as Guilds in the Middle Ages, go as far back as the 10th century B.C. This SIGN represents a great farm fraternity "The National Grange" which is still active.

Once nailed high in New England this 12' long x 20" high Sign made from a thick heavy board has a number and initials above tall black letters on their original scarred white background that could've been seen from quite a distance down the road.

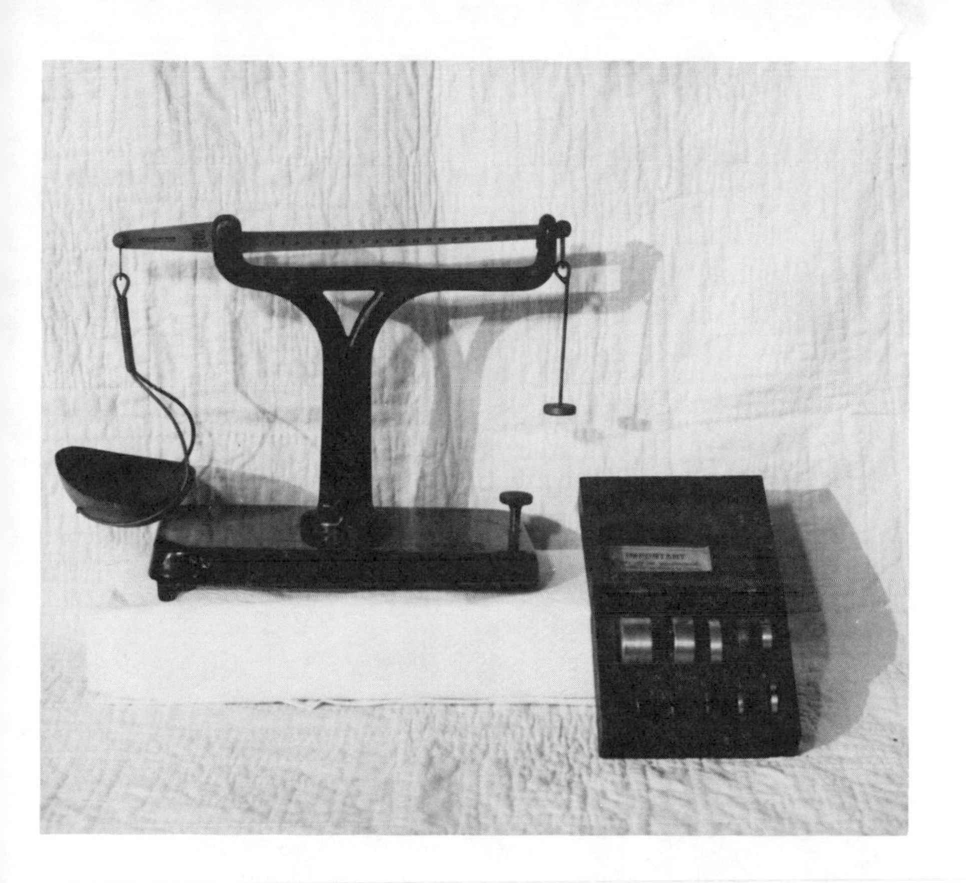

ASSAYERS' SCALE said to have been used at Dahlonega for U.S. Government purchases of gold from the miners. Gold dust and/or nuggets placed in the left tin basket were balanced by the varied-sized weights at right. If a weight was lost the manufacturer required return of the whole box unit for replacement. A tiny counter moved across the brass arm marked off the grams and a leveling screw at right plus a center base bubble made for additional accuracy.

The Georgia Goldrush centered in Dahlonega (the Indians' name for Yellow Gold) in 1832 on former Cherokee Nation Indian Lands . . . with all the tents, shacks, and gaudy paraphernalia of a typical Goldrush Town. At the old state capitol in Milledgeville a lottery wheel was set up. For a small fee any state citizen could spin, receiving 40-acre tracts numbered corresponding to those on the wheel. There were various conditions . . . a man had one chance, a widow and orphans had two chances each, and so on . . . and all had the option to sell. One recorded lot was rapidly sold for $50,000.

The big rush ended in the 1840s when prospectors and hangers-on left for California and the new strikes there, although flakes and even small nuggets are still occasionally washed from the Dahlonega streams.

Ore from the mines at Dahlonega (the Indians' name for Yellow Gold) was dumped in the top of this GOLD WASHER & SEPARATOR with its wooden Spillage guards. The broad square frame leaning beside the machine fit into the top rear. By its thin iron rod handle the frame was pushed back and forth to start the operation. Water was also piped in at the top from the nearest stream through a series of wooden troughs. It washed the raw ore with internal rotation screens, separating the dirt, rocks, and stones from the gold flakes and nuggets. Plantation.

Waterpowered through a system of WOODEN GEARS activated by the manually pushed handle, slag and dirty water ran down the lower trough and gold fell to the internal screens for hand removal. Plantation.

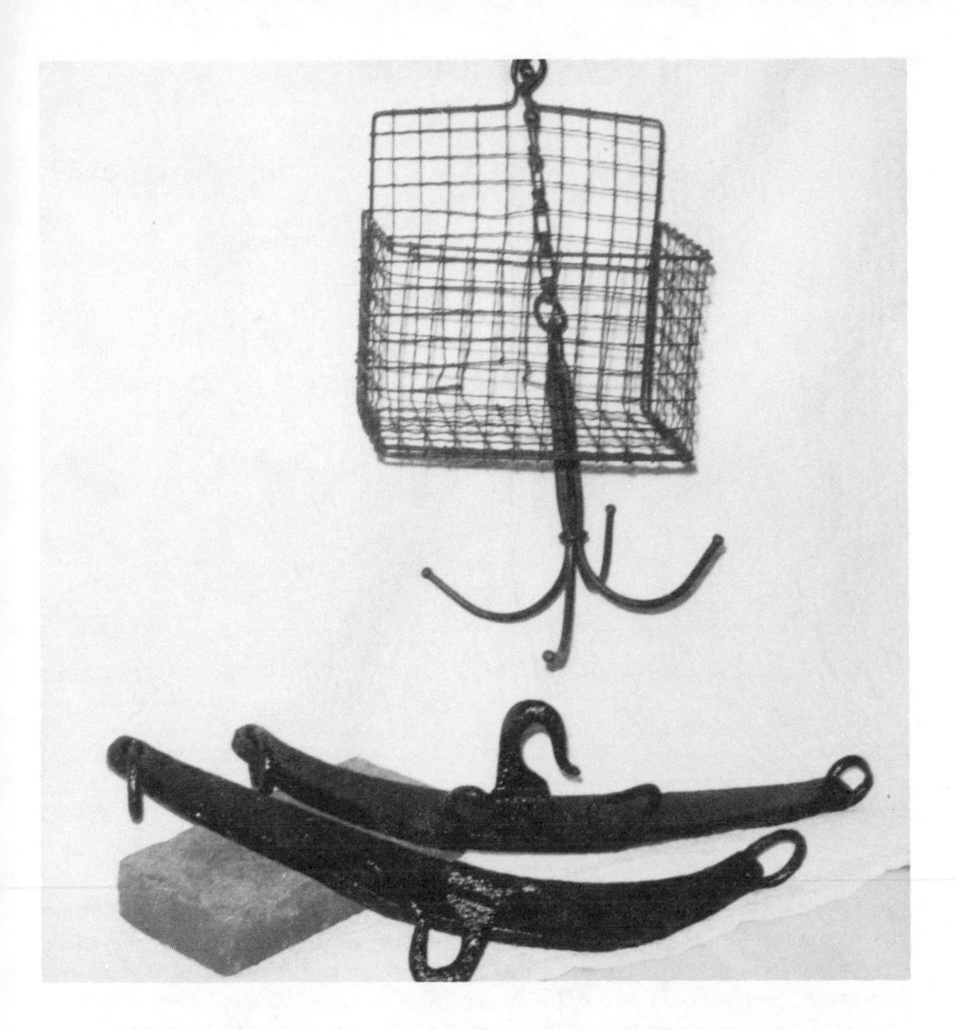

MINE LOCKER from a West Virginia Coal Mine around the late 1800s. Arriving for his shift the Miner placed his valuables and small clothes in the WIRE BASKET with his bulkier things on the knobend hooks. With the long chain slung over a high beam he pulled down the top ring which raised the Basket close to the ceiling, padlocking the ring to his allotted space on another board about 3 feet up from the floor.

After work he used his key, slipped the chain upwards and so lowered his belongings. It was ingenuous security and kept his clothes high and dry and reasonably safe from rodents.

The extra-heavy iron MINE HAMES of the same period (also made of such woods as oak and hickory) so weighted the animals' necks they were forced to keep their heads down to spare bumping against the roof supports of the low tunnels as they pulled the mine cars in and out of the underground passages . . . a debatable advantage.

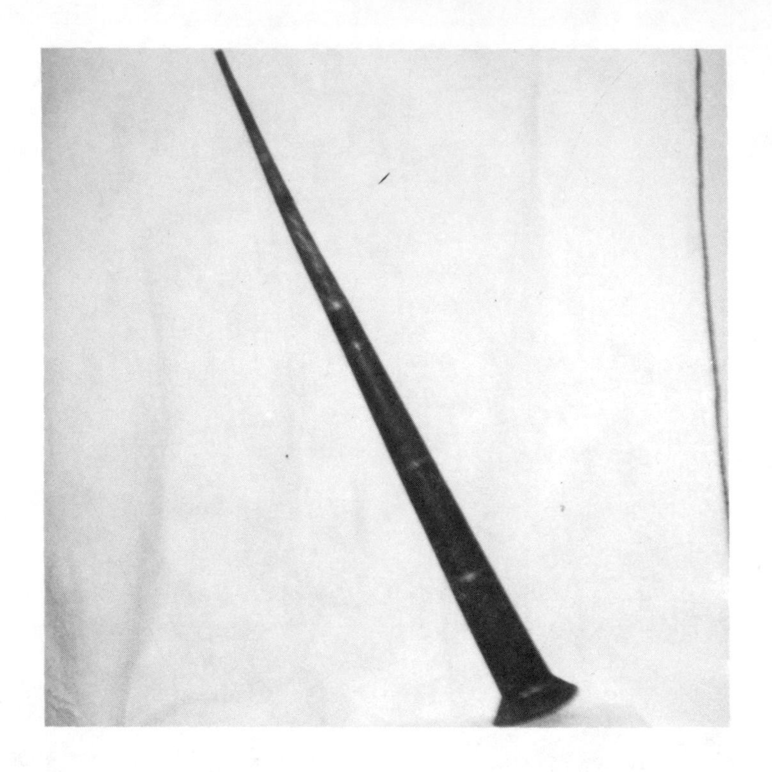

As the Stagecoach driver once started down the last of the hills coming into Macon, Georgia he blew a resounding blast on this long brass STAGECOACH HORN (approx. 36") to alert the Innkeeper of the hostel he was approaching to be ready to receive guests. A lookout lad scurried inside with the news so that upon arrival hot water and towels would be at hand, food awaiting serving, and rooms given a last "look" for possible "layovers". The Horn made in sections was fastened with brass bands. ca.: earlier 1800s.

AROUND THE BARN

About 135 years ago in central Georgia these LOGS with shaping marks were keycut to form mortise and tenon joints, locking them together as the base of a BARN. Chinked with local red clay, if tipped over by a furious wind the Barn would not collapse and could be set upright without damage to its walls. Tearing it down would entail removing the key log at the top, unwinding one by one in reverse to its raising. Plantation.

(The mortise, as seen in the preceding picture, is the cavity or cut into which the tenon is fit, the tenon first being cut and shaped for insertion.)

The BARN'S UPPER HAYMOW customarily used for hay, bags of oats and other grains, (a favorite place for children's games) has RANDOM WIDTH BOARDS with squared nails. It is possible the upper floor was added to the lower log section at a later date as usage expanded. ca.: 1840s. Plantation.

Roof shakes split with a froe and mallet were wedged in with blows from this early 1800s SHAKES HAMMER. Cut from a solid walnut block into a rounded base it has shallow nicks on only one side, and with the knob handle fitting a certain-size hand, it was obviously used by a single owner.

A grooved 1-piece oak FROE MALLET sharply struck iron FROES and with a twist of the wrist the shakes were rived off. Each single iron turned to form the handle eye was then fastened with iron rivets or simply forge-hammered flat. Every thrifty landowner had several Froes to keep a supply of shingles on hand and although Granddad could make them while seated it became a popular rainy day event for all the menfolks. Among the first of the pioneer tools Froes were replaced with sawcutting for clapboards, shakes, and so on.

One 10" diameter log gave about five 1" clapboards, and in building these were lapped about 1" or so to keep out weather. The top Froe and Mallet below were used in the 1700s and the other Froe is a bit later. Such clapboards were used in America far into the 1800s.

A real gem is this squared poll (head) AMERICAN GOOSEWING BROADAXE from the 1700s, named for its graceful birdswing curve, held with both hands for hewing round logs into square beams. A Pennsylvania blacksmith forged steel to the iron base rim for strength and to longer hold a keener edge. Repeatedly hefting the Axe he achieved the period-typical straight handle cut to his exact grip. The unusual blade guard is a canoe-like hollowed wooden cradle. For his personal touchmark he punctured the iron when still hot with a square nail he had undoubtedly also made, all this meticulous attention giving us far beyond practicality a glimpse of his striving for perfection . . . and artistry in iron.

A PINDRILL ca.: 1800s is a heavy iron wood base TOOL handcranked on each side handle causing gears to rotate various size drills below that bored holes for wooden pins used in building. (Downs).

The right IRON STAR has flaking original mustard yellow paint. It is quite heavy; fastened to a Pennsylvania Dutch barn about 1840 it had a dual purpose. It was a HEX SIGN to ward off evil, and in the same way as the lower iron STAR served during the 1850s on a brick building in St. Louis, it helped firm the stone structure. A long iron pole inside just under the roof went through the walls, each end bolted through the center of a Star on the outside to hold the walls straight up . . . from leaning. The Stars were ornamental as well as practical. A few still remain.

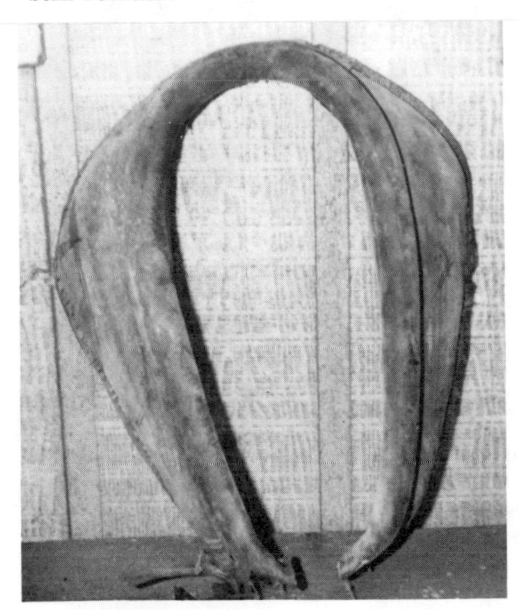

An early strawpacked-hard leather HORSE-COLLAR. In buying look for those with stitching intact. (Downs).

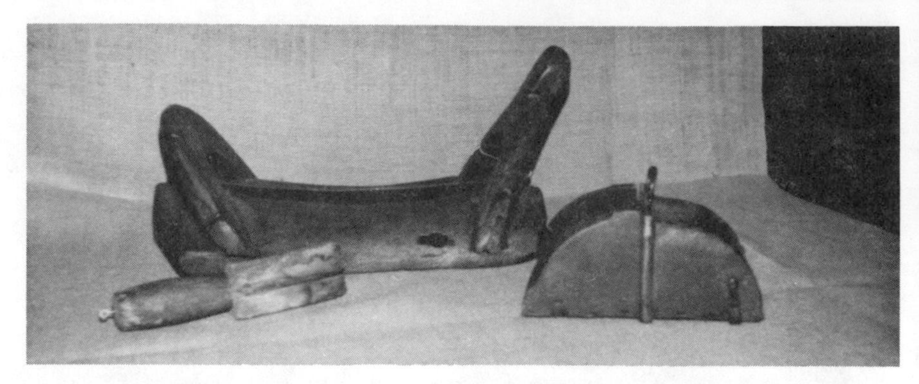

A wooden PACKSADDLE ca.: 1840 has side openings for straps to hold packs of goods, these balanced at the animals' sides for easier carrying.

An interesting STIRRUP ca.: early 1800s from our southwestern regions has brass sides and a brass foothold band with a closed wooden front to protect the rider's foot from thorny chaparral and such.

In the 1800s this small 1-piece handcut wooden TOOL was used to smooth MORTAR between bricks in building.

A thick farm-made 8' long oak board with 1" dia. wooden pins that fit tightly into auger-bored holes hung on the inside wall of a barn as a PINBOARD, holding whatever was necessary. In a today's shop it has a BRIDLE with blinder, a BARN LANTERN, and a hand-fashioned hickory RAKE with six crudely whittled pegs as teeth. Left is a wire MUZZLE put on a mule when weeding cornfields to prevent the animal from eating ripening ears; the right tinned sheet iron FIREBUCKET filled with water, or more often sand, hung high and was pointed at the base so a janitor at a southern thread mill could not set it on the floor as a scrub bucket . . . and in a far-northern boarding house this same style was always ready . . . also pointed to discourage "hired girls" from converting them. ca.: 1800s. (Below are miscellaneous collectibles.)

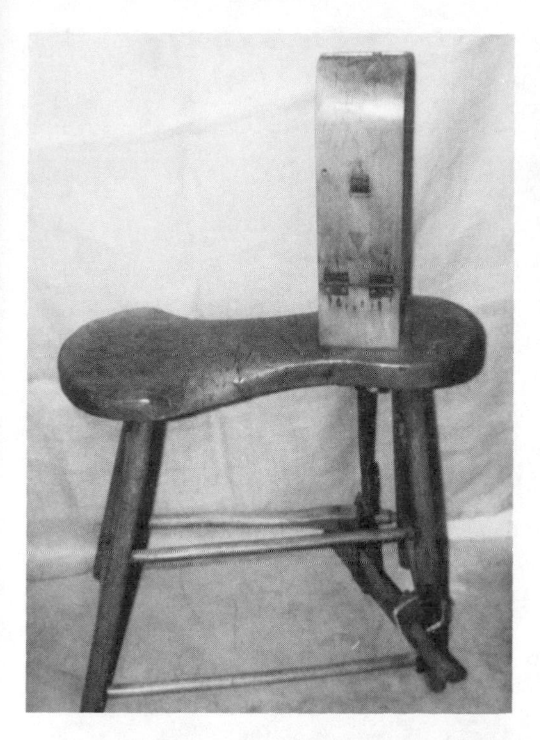

For ease of operation a worker seated on the saddle of this hickory HARNESS STITCHER controlled by a foot lever (l. frt. rt.) a wide strap which caused the big wooden pincers to firmly secure leather intended for new-fashioning or for repairs. ca.: 1830-40.

Dough Chest c:1850. Pine handfashioned in Virginia. Pegged 6 -board construction; sides continue into unusual lyre-type graceful legs. Unhinged top is decoratively grooved with 3 narrow wood rails added to position and secure the lid.

In faraway Buttermilk Valley in the Georgia Hills this LIGHTWAGON WHEEL lay partially covered with drifted leaves and pine needles; close by were stands of blackeyed daisies and the ruins of a century-old cabin stubbornly holding on. The Wheel, of course, is beyond repair but if it were not it would be difficult to have rebuilt due to the inadequacies of materials and tools and skills no longer sought. The wooden rim where not decayed is still solid against the forged iron tire and with so much left after its long weathering the Wheel speaks of prideful blacksmithing.

The SHOP SIGN was farther down the trace in an abandoned lean-to.

One type of FARMWAGON used with BANGBOARDS . . . in the old days of handhusking corn in the fields a temporary high board was mounted on the far side of the Wagon . . . from this the ears of corn tossed by the Huskers rebounded into the Wagon, resulting in those boards being called "BANGBOARDS" . . . (the Huskers did not need to turn and look each time they threw over their shoulders). (Downs).

The upper half of a FIFTH WHEEL from a 4-wheeled carriage (also used on such as 4-wheeled wagons, buggies) prevented scooting or skidding of the front wheels in turning. Here two half-circular pieces of red-painted iron and plain hickory wood were face to face, the top portion mounted to the body, the lower mating portion attached to the axle. As the vehicle turned, the Fifth Wheel allowed the horse (or team) to turn the conveyance very sharply to the left or right without tipping. The weight and size of the Wheel was determined by the weight and size of the vehicle. This same principle is used in modern version on tractor-trailers that daily ride our highways. ca.: 1800s.

When one in a team of freight wagons, for instance, became stuck on a hill, in a mudhole, or crossing a stony creekbed a second team of mules (or horses) could strengthen the first using this early 1800s smithy-made STRETCHER.

Its heavy top iron was hooked over the center ringbolt of the doubletree and harnesses fastened onto the lower open points below the hickory sapling crossbar, the latter held with bentover forged nails. (This wood quickly wore out under severe weight and pulling but was no problem to frugally replace with so many trees about.)

Hinged iron side tugs permitted easier turning.

Once the wagon was free and again in line it was simple to unhook the Stretcher and reharness the temporary team to its own wagon.

For curbing unruly hard-mouthed mules the double-ring top iron BIT is spiralled, the lower tightly curled, both worn thin from contact with big teeth and smithy-fashioned in the 1800s.

Only oxen were strong and patient enough to endure this hand-fashioned huge hickory DOUBLE YOKE. With the curved part of the top they pulled with their heavy necks, nature assisting by building up a thick callous. Usually amenable to the driver's voice in gentle urging, if thirsty and they smelled water, the animals just took off. Preferred over horses and mules in clearing rough and hilly lands and for hauling big loads, they could also be harnessed for transportation of family and goods. With their tails tied together to hold them in position, and a horse tied in front to show them how to pull, young oxen were winter-trained for readiness at spring-plowing time. ca.: 1700s.

The smaller GOAT YOKE is bentwood pierced with an iron bolt. Giving adequate restraint it permitted the animals to graze.

These date in the mid-1800s although similar were used long before and after.

One of the first GREASE BUCKETS 7" diameter x 9" tall sheet iron (to replace more vulnerable wooden ones made from hollowed out logs) that hung on the axles of covered wagons. Also, rather than slush, this used axle grease with tar added to prevent its melting during hot weather, the grease applied with a stick rammed down into the gaumey mess to lubricate the hubs and axles. Rivets hold the lid inside the folded over top and bottom and permit it to swing back and forth. As a standard artillery implement, during the 1860s this rare tool hung by its forged iron chain on the limbers and caissons.

The single young OXEN TRAINER left is worn with its heavier side up and over the big neck at the shoulder. Training began in ample time for the calves to be ready for breaking to a plow.

Beside it the COW HALTER has lost its center Poke.

A handcrafted pair of walnut WORKHOUSE HAMES was used in harnessing for heavy chores. Fastened either side and slightly in front of the collar, the latter acted as a shoulder cushion from the pull of the Hames.

The next oblong type YOKE retains its long POKE which caught in a barrier if the animal tried to jump or push out of an enclosure. The curved YOKE which opens at both ends held by wooden pegs has long wooden pins for the purpose of the POKE. Even certain flighty hens wore tiny wooden yokes to hold them down rather than have their wing feathers clipped.

The left WAGONHAMMER joined the singletree to the wagon. Its square jaws fit the big nuts holding the wheel to the axle and the back of the jaws was the Hammer. The long rosetop JOINER SPIKE performed the single task of holding. Each handle has a deeply worn notch from contact with the large implements they joined, both forged mid-1800s.

An oak WAGON JACK with a right moving roller. The arm at left placed up and parallel to the ground, the Jack grooves put in position under the wagon axle at the required height slot, and the arm then clamped down held the Jack firm as repairs were being made. Around mid-1800s.

At right, showing how large is the Jack, a pre-1850 WHEELWRIGHTS' and COACHMAKERS' SPOKE POINTER & TRIMMER has its original replaceable steel blade, and slightly tapered and trimmed wooden wheel spokes.

An outstanding example of a homemade primitive from the late 1700s - early 1800s is this heavy wooden GRAIN CARRIER of 1" thick boards 12" deep, square nails holding the water-softened and bent handle taut, bark age-hardened on the branch. Filled, it must-ve been heavy t' tote.

A 75 lbs. SEA ISLANDS RICE POUNDER during the 1700s could have also been used as needed for other grains. Time has chomped away at one outerbase side of the inside-oval MORTAR. The POUNDING STICK (PESTLE) held when used in both hands shows greater wear at one end, this and the Mortar each cut from its individual block of hard pine.

A STORAGE BARREL cut from a hollow cypress log with an added flat wooden base held grains to be transferred to individual manger feed boxes with scoops and wooden shovels. ca.: 1840-50. Plantation.

A TACKLE BLOCK with its single rope wood pulley was for hauling up heavy loads as hay and grains into the barn loft. Often it held the rope in dragging vehicles out of mudholes.

The iron HAND CORN-SHELLER was patent dated over a hundred years ago at a Cincinnati, Ohio shop. It hinged over the knuckles in three sections fastened with leather straps and the projecting burrs removed the kernels as the ear was dragged across.

A homemade wood and iron TOOL with peg holes for positioning the adjustable handle to "scrape" the blade back and forth; much conjecture . . . nothing for certain. (Downs).

A GRINDSTONE (Grinding Wheel) ca.: 1860 was for sharpening any dull farm tool. Handturned with a crank (which was often soon lost and a stick through the spokes substituted), a drip cup of water kept the stone moistened to afford a keener edge. (Downs).

Often called "The Connecticut" this heavy sharp HAYKNIFE was found in its wooden shipping case in a closed New England warehouse. Used to saw out from the stack any given amount of hay needed for feeding, they could have been termed HAYSAWS. Here the top is painted red with silver below. Latter 1800s.

A husky MILKING STOOL handcut from green oak was 1800s used. Tops of the smoothed branch legs split at the seat end had wood wedges inserted for extra strength, this method often seen in early construction.

The seam-lapped brass COWBELLS have carved wooden clappers. Whittled pins hold the rough-stitched leather collars, the O. Star mark on the top bell is Michigan origin, and each has an individual melodious tone. While it is an ageless belief that cows produce better milk in larger quantities to music, they could be more easily found when they wandered off on free range.

Bells have forever been an integral part of our culture and as concerned herein with rural usage . . . mules wore large round bells often 5" in diameter with holes in the sides and an interior bell clanking around; only the leader of a flock of sheep wore a rather deeply melodious bell; the billygoat wore a shrill bell while the nanny had a smaller one somewhat higher pitched; turkeys wore tiny bells about 1" in diameter.

In the early 1800s Conestoga Wagons carried on each horse a set of three to five cone-shaped brass bells mounted on a solid iron strap. If a wagon broke down or became mired and needed help the wagoner had to hand over the strands in payment. "I'll be there with bells on" is said by many to have originated with these men who would do everything humanly possible to overcome trail hazards in order to fulfill the boasts of arriving with all bells jingling and intact.

Commonly called "tiger" maple is a natural branch 3-legged MILKING STOOL ca.: early 1800s which is still almost as durable as when it was made, having slash-pegged leg tops extending through the seat.

For a long time pioneers had only home remedies for sick or injured domestic animals. In the 1850s a certain Cow Doctor (title courtesy to his knack) had a handyman who helped in "doctorin' th' toucheous patients" using this handcrafted maple DRENCHER ASISST or NOSE TWISTER. Placed over th' critter's head just above the nostrils the rope was twisted for control while Doc administered th' cures. Also, when the center round with a funnel inserted was placed in the mouth, tonics could be poured down the animal's throat while the side rounds acted as handyman handholds to steady it and keep the mouth open. Not a fancy medical appliance (it still shows pencil marks from laying out) it was effective and not too hard on the patients.

Farther along in the 1800s another handy Cow Doctor used this improved DRENCHING BIT patented in St. Louis. Athollow iron fastened for control to the animal's chest rein by the two links below. With the straight bit in its mouth and the frame pulled back over its nose and head medicine poured into the left tall funnel ran down and into the mouth through a hole in the middle of the mouth bit, not too rapidly to cause choking. It was a humane and fairly sure way of getting the intended cure into the alarmed critter's throat.

Before 1860 this homemade VISE was used on its particular homestead for top-patchin' high boots although it might also have served for harness-hold mending, the left pincers end opened and closed by raising and lowering the handle. (Plantation).

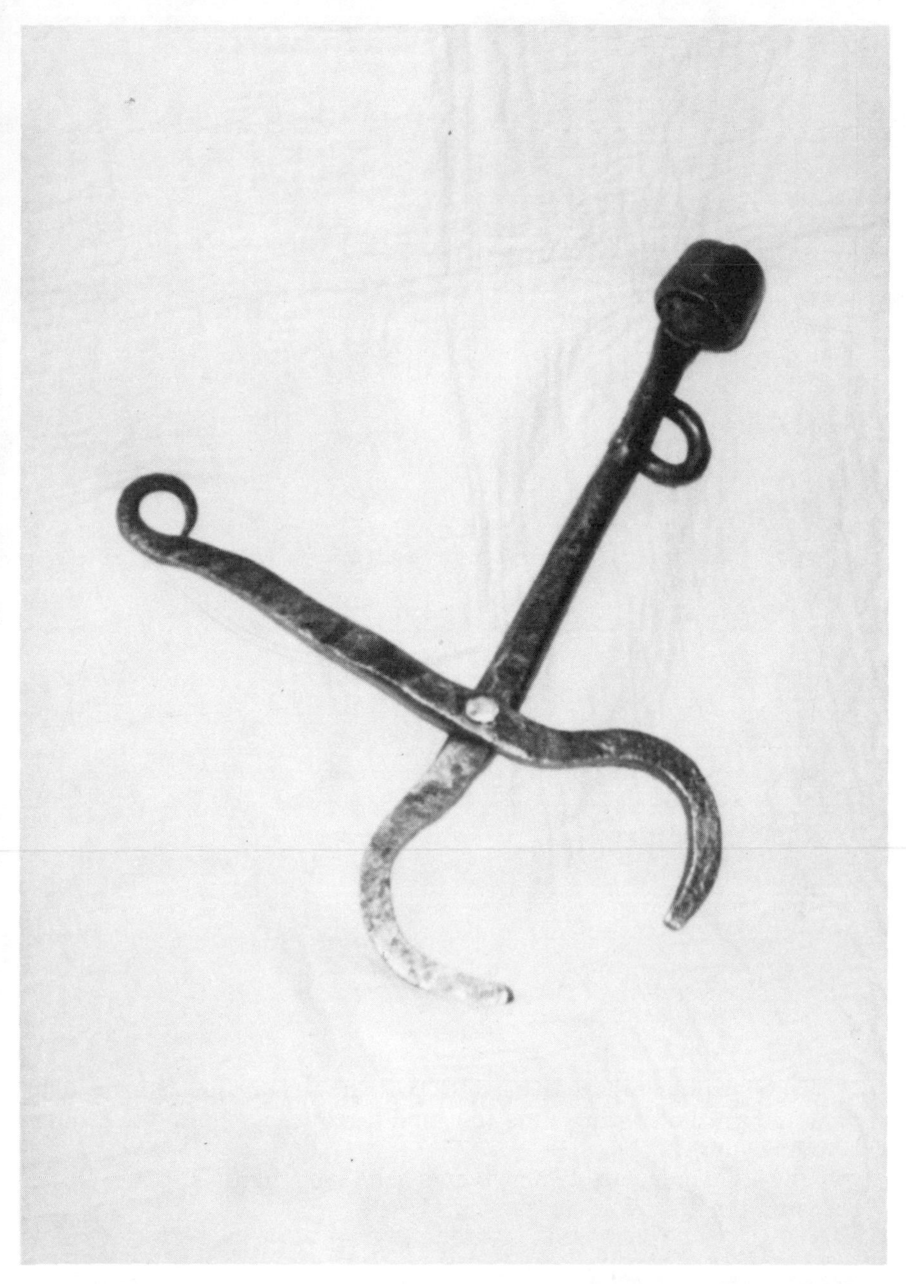

Before 1850 here is one blacksmith's idea of an iron PIGCATCHER to grab a squealing porker by a hind leg. Application required a branch pole stuck into the lower right cup, a rope through the rings, a strong arm, a quick eye, nimble footwork . . . and good eardrums. Effective it was.

Three handcut oak HOGSTRETCHERS (Gamb'lin' Sticks) held firm at farm butchering time the hind legs of hogs hung for cooling before cutting.

The still-very-sharp Pennsylvania handwrought FOODCHOPPERS prepared the meat for sausage. ca.: 1870s.

Two wide wooden pincers iron hinged and a smaller at left held with leather are 1800s CRACKLIN' SQUEEZERS that pressed drops of lard from pork scraps floating up in th' renderin' kettles, the bits having been put first into cloth bags. The result was crisp cracklin's good to eat plain or baked in cornbread.

Of an earlier date in the same century, tinner-made from one piece of tin riveted onto its original wooden handle in this GREASE DIPPER which skimmed and dipped the bubbling fat. At center is a handcut HOGSTRETCHER of the same period.

These heartpine hand-adzed STAIRS are impervious to insects but will quickly burn. Hay or cornshucks spread out in the loft and laid over with kiver-quilts or meal sacks stuffed with any available cotton made warm whispery pallets fer th' younguns. "An' when ther wuz a gatherin' th' lil tykes hung over a'gapin' an' a'starin' bugeyed frum th' hole at th' top a th' ladder." As geese became obtainable their feathers were saved for highly prized and much softer mattress innards. ca.: 1840-50. Plantation.

An iron BEDWARMER with an iron handle and open ring for hanging has a punched decorative copper lid and an iron liftknob. ca.: 1860.

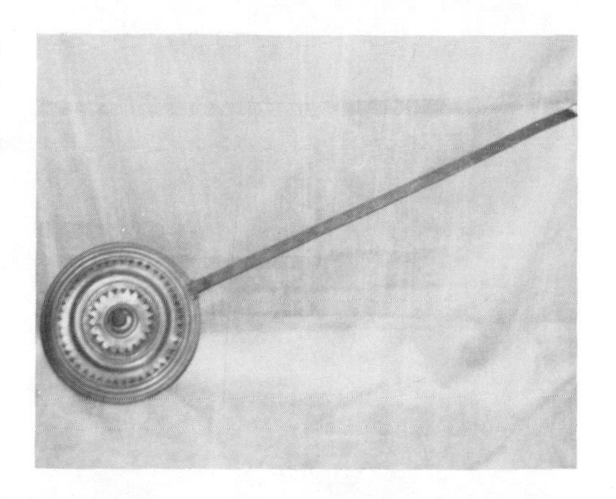

An outstanding handcrafted knotty pine STOOL from upper New York State in the 1700s. Of 3 wideboard construction, sides extend as wedges into the seat slash-pegged for strength. In Shaker fashion the stretcher is mortised into the sides, each base having prideful irregular scallops. The felling of a stately tree was muted by the beauty and convenience its one small part introduced into a stark frontier cabin.

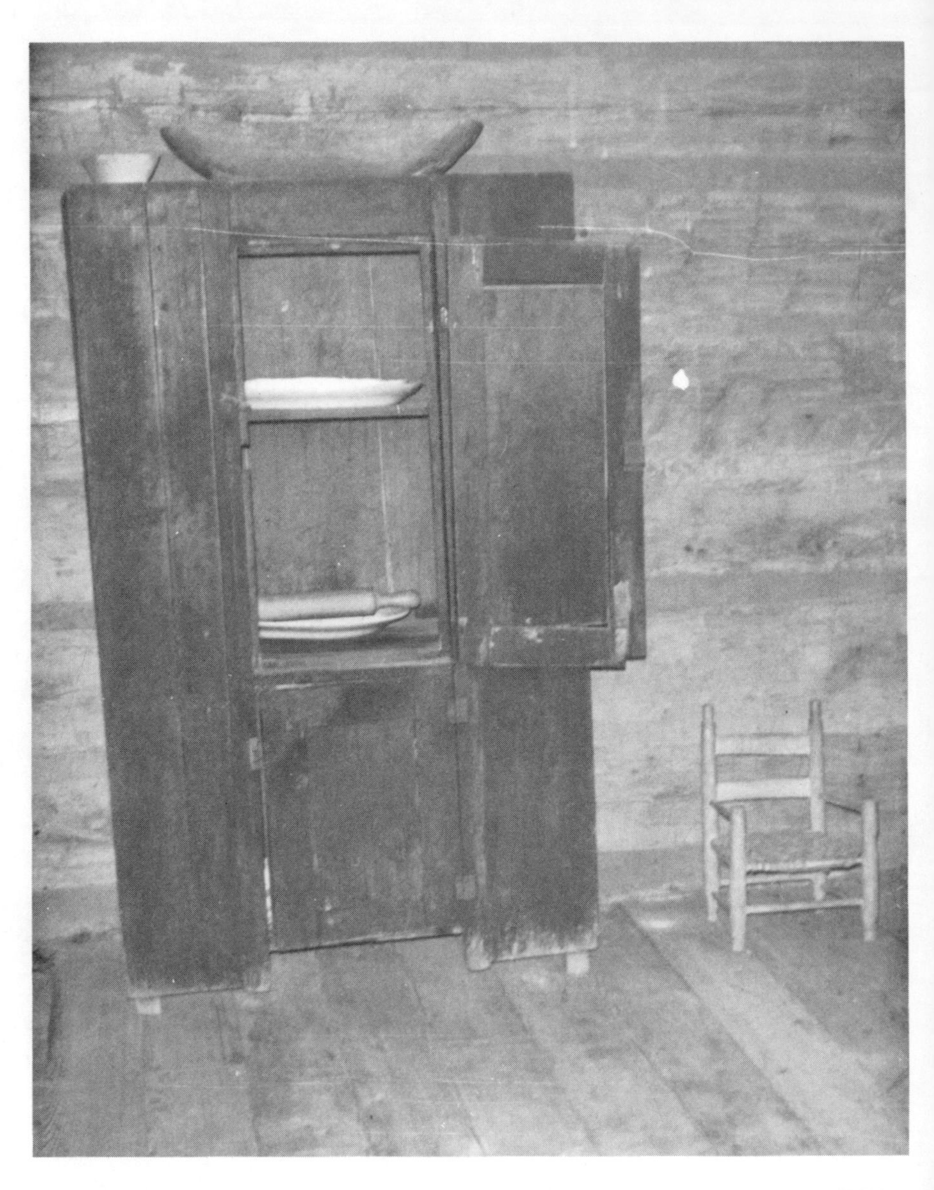

Beside a child's woven rushseat CHAIR blocks assist a pine CUPBOARD of random width boards struggling with an original left side list, age, and a sloping floor to remain upright. On a day before 1845 a sweating Mister with more grit that ability provided this luxury fer th' Missus. Her almost-certain surprise at its curious slants would have been immediately forgotten in her overwhelming pride and gratitude. With forged iron hinges its upper and lower solid doors open by plain-cut wood "knobs", each having a forged nail driven through and bent over inside the door. Plantation.

A poplar ROCKING CHAIR made for a cabin long before 1840 could've "jis sorta got t'gether an' wuz shur a site-comfertable"; perhaps first a straight chair with its low front and back stretchers, later-added rear leg braces, and arms too low for comfort raised with thin wood rests grooved for decoration on the outer sides.

Note the period-typical stubby rocker-front projections and the way in which the wide legs are half-socketed onto them. The high solid back was a fine headrest and kept out drafts. (Plantation).

The overlarge tinner-made CUP with lapped edges folded at top and bottom and applied wide handle dates from the latter 1700's. A member of the same family continued using it in the Civil War for food rations, drinking and washing water, and doing small laundry. Here it holds POPCORN BERRIES still being sold as they were over a hundred years ago on the streets of Charleston, S.C.

A 5-board cherry CRICKET dates about 1790. From colonial times to the cabins of the last Settlers everyone feared the dangerously chilling drafts that swept over the floors and kept their feet up whenever possible.

About 1830 in the Ohio Territories pricked fingers sewed patches for remembrance into a now-softly faded QUILT. Several generations felt they could fall asleep only if dragged down by at least one thick-padded cotton "Comfort" with quilt overlays "that'd make yer limbs give out afore th' sun ud even kum up".

A familiar kerosene WALL LAMP in its tin holder flickered in most kitchens . . . anywhere it was needed.

A rope BEADSTEAD might have been a treasured piece that "kum down an' bin keerfully toted in a wagon on th' fearsum journey" to a strange new homestead, there to also serve as a Settin' Bench. This custom prevailed too in finer homes where the master bedroom door opened off the entry. With a table, chairs, and such the room became a second, or Ladies' Parlor, where the bed under a formal daytime covering gave extra seating for an overflow from the Gentlemen's Parlor. It took about 120 ft. of rope to lace a bed, this periodically twist-tightened to keep it taut with a homemade wooden device known as a Bed Key, this latter to no special pattern but according to the maker's ideas; oddly enough all ended up looking like giant clothespins with handlebars. ca.: 1840-50. Plantation.

Pioneer brides believed small grey spiders spinning cobwebs in the dim dusty corners overhead brought good luck to their cabins and did not brush the webs away.

An early copper WATER PITCHER and BOWL set has an interestingly deep basin with pouring spout and slim handle on the Pitcher uncommonly proportioned to its overall size. ca.: 1870. Courtesy Murfreesboro, Tennessee Antique Mall.

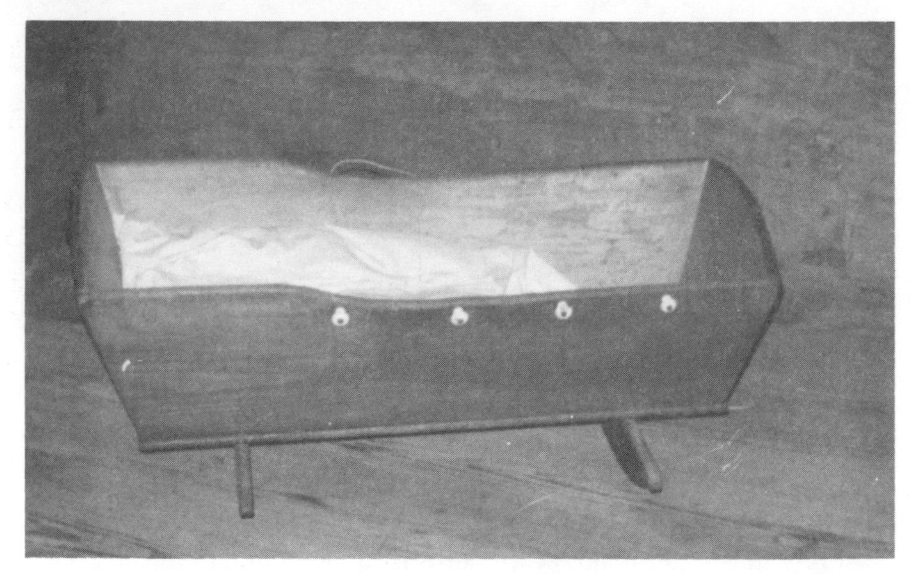

PINE CRADLE with china knobs place-made in the 1800s. If the child needed to be briefly unattended a thin rope laced across the cradle top, fastened to the rosettes, forestalled its falling or crawling out. If baby was old enough to thrash about, a rattle or other small toy was tied to the ropes for a jingling distraction. Plantation.

From the early 1700s a RUSHLIGHT HOLDER of blacksmith fashioned iron and a hardwood block held rushes folded in such a way that when inserted in the pincers they straightened out under fairly rapid burning. This ancient form of lighting was used by our first settlers, to some extent by the Pilgrims. Common reeds as cattails native to swampy areas were peeled to the spine (pith), saturated with melted grease in a long container, pressed together, and hung in bunches to dry. Until cattle were brought into this country in numbers after the mid-1600s deer and bear fats were most frequently used. Note the successful attempt to "mek ut purty", with two rings spaced around the lower part of the iron, the matching two cut below the top of the base, and the button knob wrought on the handle.

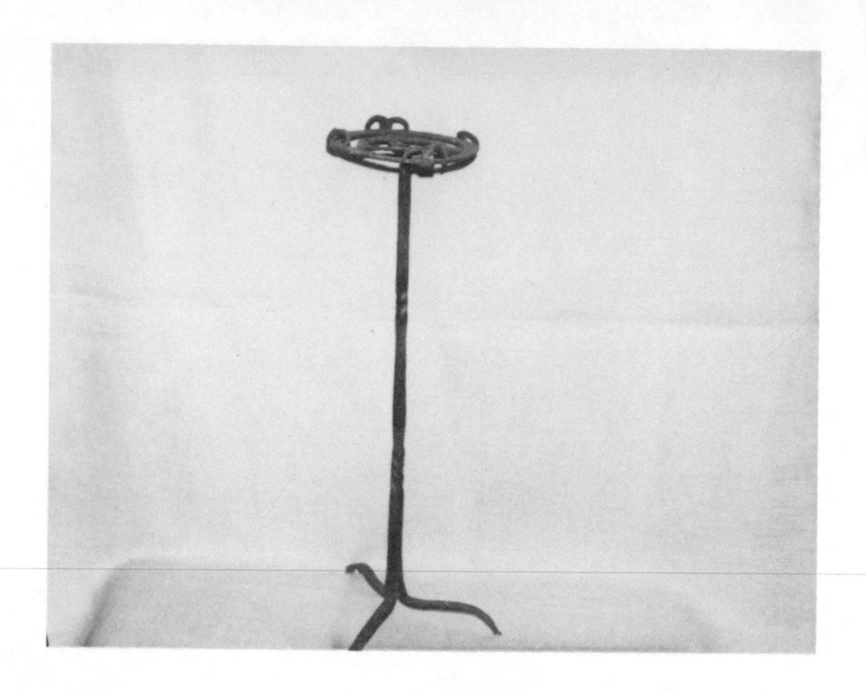

This CRESSET, an example of skillful blacksmithing, is one piece of iron heated, pounded, and wrought into a twisted pedestal stand, the base split into three pronged feet, each having its own curve and dimension but all finally level. The top continues into a rosette holding the round burner; two crosspieces extended at either end, bent into loops, three double and one single although the last was made that way so it must have been the last piece of iron left right then to finish up the burner. On these are forged two circles, the smaller inside and the outer touching the rim scallops, both forged to the crossbars.

A Cresset, an iron framework in several forms, is an early lighting device, a variation of simple firebaskets. It burned pitchy wood from resinous trees as pineknots in the northeast and candlewood in the southwest. It could stand as here, be used as a torch or hung as a lantern. In the home it carried fire from room to room, outside from house to house; could be carried on a pole to light the way through dark passageways for pedestrians and carriages.   early 1700s.

PAN LAMPS (Cruisies) of iron were made and used in America for over 200 years, these from the 1700s. A step from rushlights a forged saucer was bent to form shallow corners that held one to four twisted cotton or rag wicks, and one end in a corner, the other in the grease at center. Hung over chairbacks for light, stuck into chinks in cabin walls or between fireplace stones they were handy for peering into cooking pots. The pointed spear could act as a wickpick to remove carbon at the burning end or loosen the wick when it became stuck. In the 1600s with fish oils first used along our northeastern coasts lamps were often hung at the front of the hearth so drafts could carry obnoxious odors up the chimney.

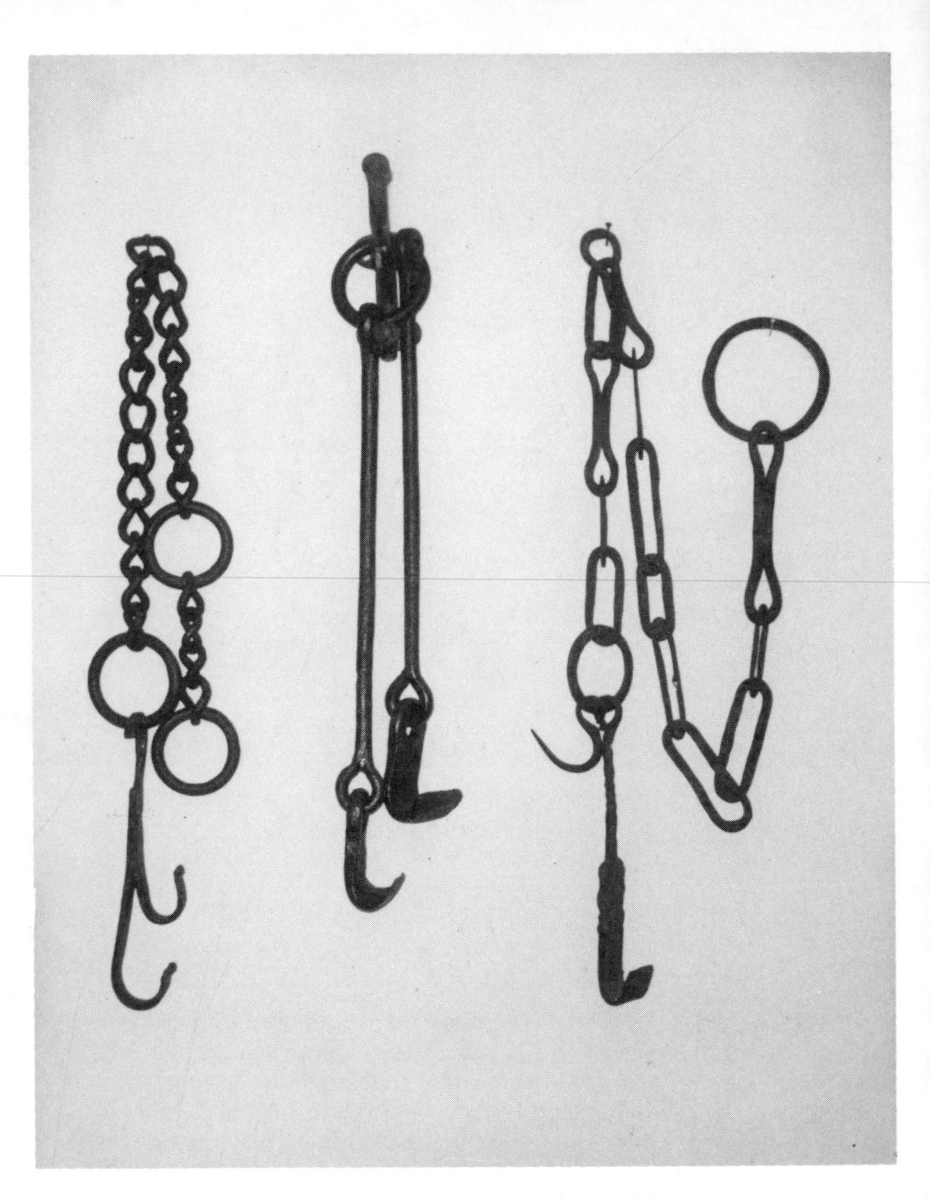

Of these 1700s TRAMMEL HOOKS three hung on their long chains from hooks imbedded in the top of the fireplace opening to hold steaming pots and kettles over the coals. The oldest, right, with an extra curved spear to hold light cuts of meat has the blacksmith's special touch in being artfully twisted; the rare left has an unusual chain; the heavy pair of center Hooks hung from a side swinging crane, although with looping the other two could have been similarly suspended. swinging crane, although with looping the other three could have been similarly suspended.

Cast in sand these 1700s ANDIRONS (FIRE DOGS) were able to hold good-sized logs. They have the typical open ring design of their period.

A tinner's skill is noted in the COFFEE POT with its curled knob and lapped edges; the copper bottom still solid with few dents since the 1840s.

A blacksmith-fashioned iron TRIVET early 1800s was convenient with its movable handlerest for keeping the contents of pots and pans warm over the fireplace coals raked out onto the hearth, even accommodating the very long handles of the big skillets.

A 42" piece of green oak showing quartered at one edge was handfashioned about 1810 into an oven PEEL 18" round. The handle is cut off-center and the lower right side is scorched; used to lift loaves of bread in and out of brick beehive ovens built in the sides of early fireplaces used for cooking as well as heating.

A handcut 1-piece sycamore DOUGHCUTTER has attractive graining similar to tiger maple. c: 1800.

A brass COOKING POT with a hanging ring in its iron handle has an iron tilting hold on the opposite side. ca.: 1850.

Auger-bored holes in a thick rough slab with a handle inserted at an angle was the MOP, this laid on a rock to "drene". Dried cornshucks folded over were tightly wedged into the sections, the rougher fold side protruding at the bottom. With sand as the abrasive scrubbing a puncheon floor "left y' plumb tuckered out but it wuz wet an' felt a site better". Such Mops continued for many years, even well into this century in isolated areas.

Flanked by tin DIPPERS used for liquids as water and milk is a castiron STEAMER or century-ago DOUBLE BOILER. Filled with water and set over the fireplace coals or on a stove it heated the contents of a smaller (usually iron) container fastened by its handle over a hook placed in the center of the heart indentation.

A handsomely rare BEEHIVE OVEN FRONT blacksmith made in Pennsylvania around 1820 has an overlong swing handle with a bulbous end so the hand will not be in front of the heat at opening. It is well designed with a center shield, flowers at the corners and buttons around the frame. (Abercrombie).

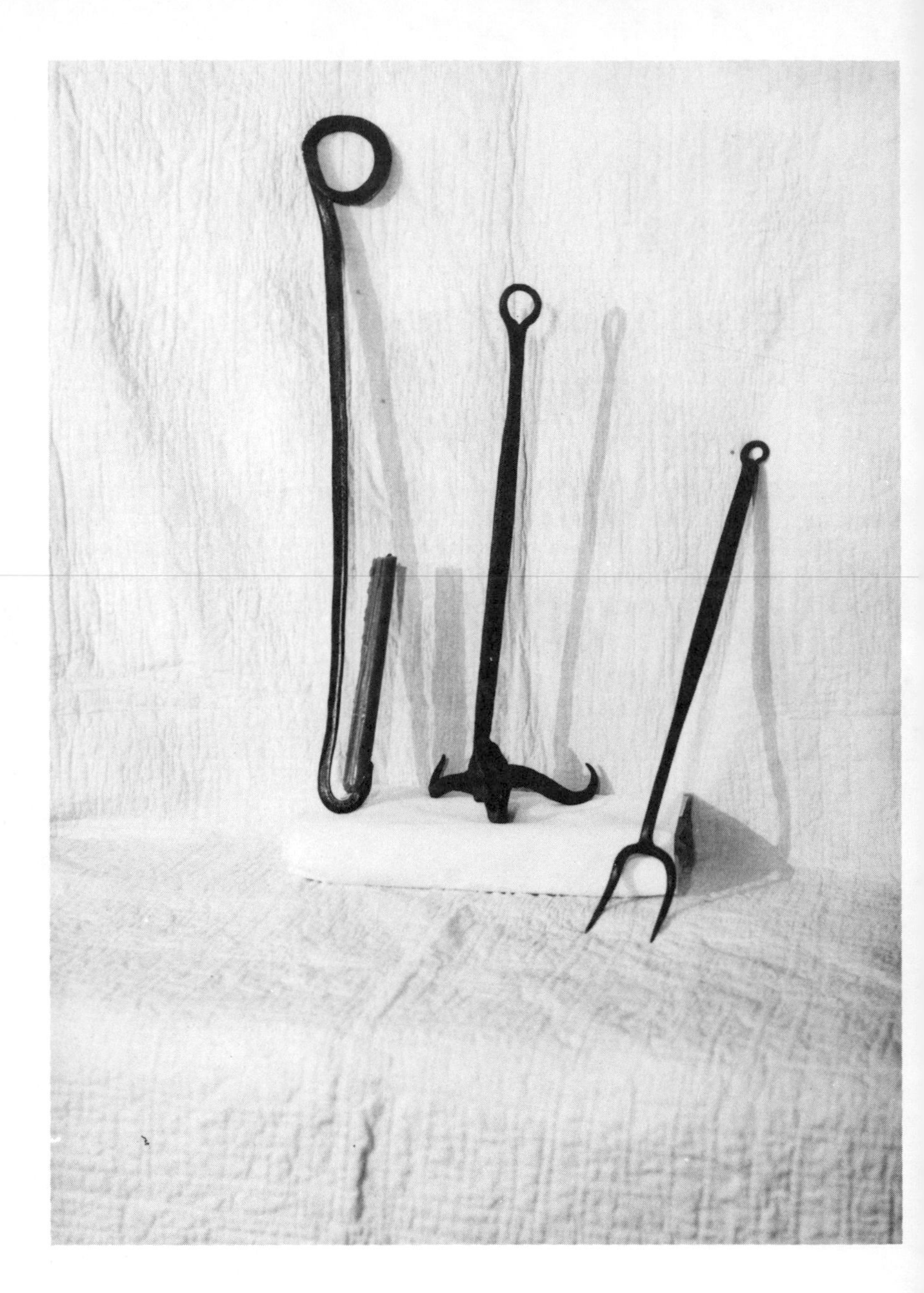

The left CANDLEHOLDER smithy-signed held light cuts of meat for fireplace roasting as well as providing a hanging light. The center MEAT PRONGS folded in a wonderfully crude and attractive manner held similar meat pieces; and with the TESTING FORK all have swirled eye tops. 1700s.

A tinned iron FOODGRATER handfashioned about 1860 and a heavy iron lidded COOKING POT of the same period are in a century younger than the handfashioned COOKING FORK and the adjustable SAWTOOTH FIREPLACE TRAMMEL dating around 1780-90, the latter's jagged style more sought after by today's collectors than those of smoother edges.

CHEESE BASKETS used for drainage are not now commonly seen. 1850 (Abercrombie).

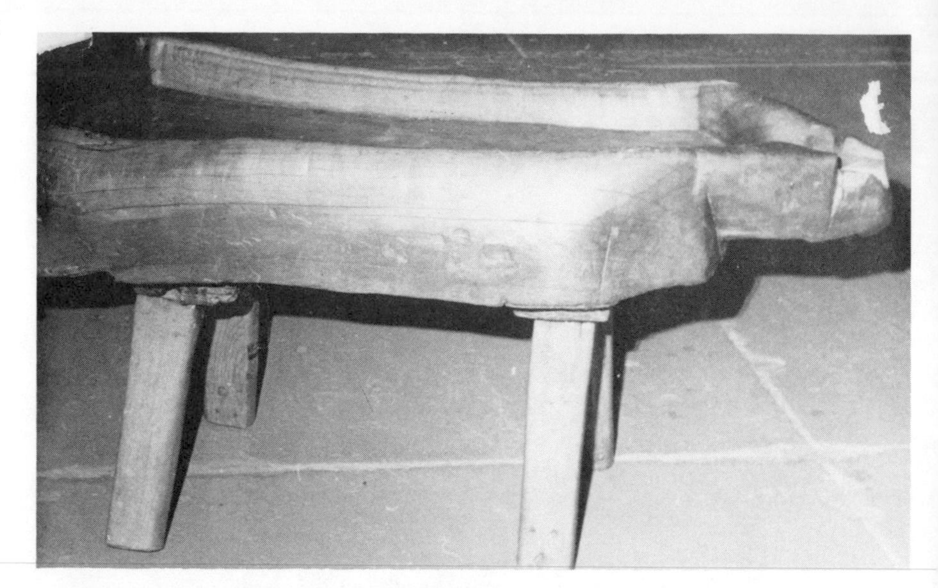

A 1-piece cedar heart CHEESE DITCH from Pennsylvania in the 1700s has a satiny-smoothed bowl and a heavily-roughcut underside. Four splay-legged hickory supports angle into deep slots held only by the considerable weight of the Ditch. Milk curds dumped into the basin were pressed and drained, the whey flowing out the trough into a wooden bucket hung in the worn slot . . . a magnificent primitive.

Rinsed with cool well water and propped in a corner of the rail fence for sundrying is a CHEESE FORD (Mold) about 1850 of 6" wide oak curve dished-inside. Its 1" thick sides are tongue and grooved with spaced wedges. As the wood aged, becoming white in usage, several square firming nails were added along with iron bands. Overall are small drainage holes. The whey that seeped from coagulated curds was fed to the pigs.

An uncommon tinned rolled sheetiron BUTTER-CHURN from around the 1850s has a metal collar to prevent milk splashing out as the poplarwood dasher was plunged up and down. Wide handles facilitate upending the churn and moving it about. With no way to measure temperature of the cream before placing it in the churn, this "b' guess 'n b' golly" method wasn't easy. Plantation.

A small wooden TUB has wrapped debarked, soaked, and sized white oak splints while a woven "market" BASKET at right with a laced rim and a regionally called "gizzard" BASKET from its shape both have bent hickory handles. (The name of a tree known in Virginia soon after 1650 as "Pohickory" stemmed from the Indians' "Pawcohiccora", meaning oil from pounded hickory nuts, later shortened to "Hickory". Courtesy Murfreesboro, Tennessee Antique Mall.

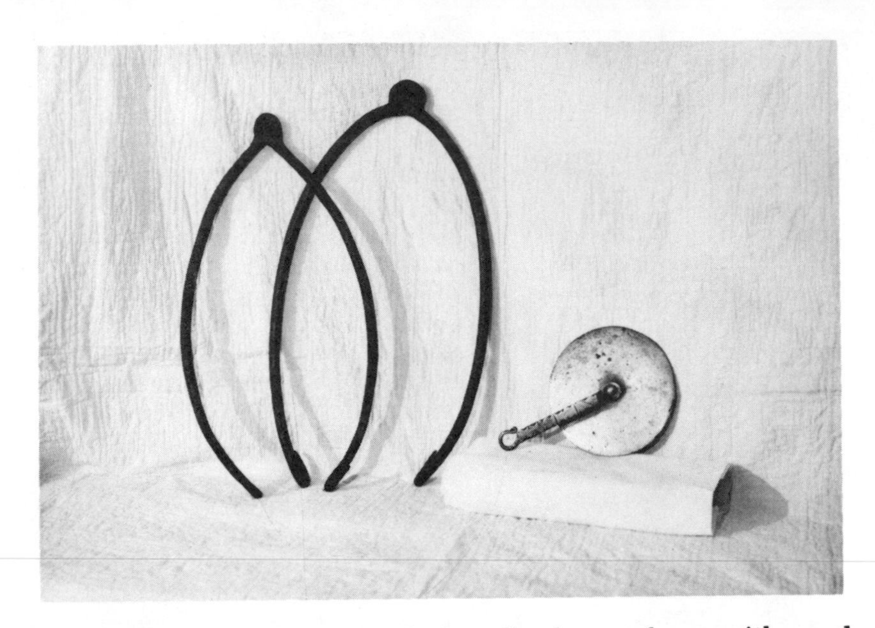

Used from the earliest to the last fireplace cookery smithy-made iron DOUBLE POTHOOKS as these around 1820 swung from trammels or side cranes holding cooking vessels.

This REVOLVING POTLID from the 1700s surely was a gift . . . its knobend rattail design handle and overall original creative work represents many arduous hours for a smithy beyond his regular chores.

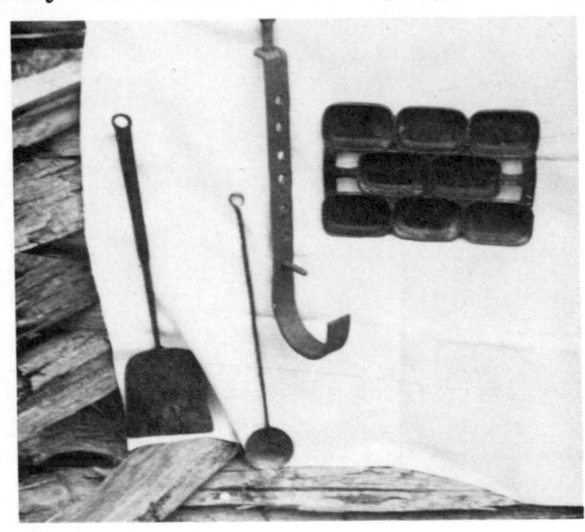

Left to right . . . wrought early 1800s . . . a PIE PEEL to slide the pastries in and out of brick ovens, bread peels having longer handles; a TASTER with a swirled top; an adjustable TRAMMEL HOOK for holding fireplace pots; and a later iron MUFFIN PAN c: 1870.

SEALING WAX CROCKS from the 1800s; the darkest a satiny brown, the center with a mark that adds to its charm, left by the potter as his touch or because in the kiln it touched a second item, the latter rubbing onto it; the Crock at right is not so plentiful. The large one below shows its hand turnings on the wheel; all are fully glazed inside and out, the largest with a deeper clay color; the inside glaze making them suitable for food storage.

For later use edibles were sealed in with the lids secured by an edge coating of thick red sealing wax, the latter cracked in required amounts from a larger slab, heated in a small iron pot kept for this purpose, and poured after melting. The wax had a pleasantly clean odor and when the food was needed the hardened wax was hit with anything handy . . . even the wooden end of a knife . . . this process predating present canning and lid sealing. These Crocks are practical and most attractive collectibles with multiple uses.

Because it made large quantities faster and was easier on the back to stand while working, this crudely homemade CABBAGE CUTTER fine-cut the vegetable for sour cabbage (sauerkraut). Its wide pitted blade is still very sharp. 1870.

A BILL HOOK (pruning knife) handcrafted in the early 1800s.

An APPLE DRYER has a cherrywood frame showing leftside sawmarks and a wire mesh center. Once pared, cored, and sliced (sometimes at Apple-Paring Bees for fun to lighten labor if there were many bushels of apples to prepare) the fruit was placed on the screen and the dryer put atop an outside shed in direct sunlight or on an inside table under a sunny window. Late 1800s.

A cherry POMACE RAKE separated the apple pomace (cheese stage) for cider making. Long whittled pins and handle were tightly wedged into auger-drilled holes. ca.: 1800 farmmade.

The small ca.: 1800 burl MORTAR and maple PESTLE were to pound and rub fine wild and cultivated yarbs (herbs) for food seasonings, dyes, and home remedies. Gardens regionally gave Hardy Sage for sausage; pineapple sage, bergamot and geranium for potpourri, jams and jellies; saffron for dyes; tansy for puddin' and pickin'; mint and basil for posy pots and taste; wormwood for liqueurs; dill, fennel, thyme, rosemary . . . all interspersed with old-timey flowers. Lavender cotton made fluffy planting borders and when cut and dried fragrantly scented clothing and linen chests. From the forests came Catnip, Slippery Ellum, Solomon's Seal, Smart Weed, Skunk Cabbage . . . all in abundance. When Ginseng could be found in quantity it was bartered to traders for coastal apothecaries and shipment to China.

Before the 1700s mustard was used only in dry powdered form stored in small pewter casters with a blind or pierced lid; it became popular as we know it during the 1700s.

A discarded chip of brick or tin placed below newly-set-out horseradish caused its hotly edible roots to spread out for better size and easier pulling.

The PESTLE could mash salt, sugar and soda carried into the home in chunks until about 1840-50.

A MORTAR 8" high x 7" diameter was handcarved from 1 piece highly desirable TIGER MAPLE. Its Honey Maple PESTLE is 12" long and skillfully carved. Both the inside oval base of the Mortar and the rounded lower end of the Pestle show considerable usage-contact, pounding and grinding all sorts of seasonings. ca.: 1700s.

A wooden WASHTUB ca.: mid-1800s has each top grip cut from one piece with the stave. Iron bands hold it firm. The inside is soap-whitened and the outside has traces of its original green.

For hundreds of years some type of SUNBONNET was standard wear, cooler in summer and warmer in winter; yet even on our earliest frontiers "th' womenfolks hankered atter fair skin" and deeply feared sunstroke. ca.: 1880.

The hickory "WASHIN' STICK" bleached at one end from homemade soap lyes made possible the stirring and lifting of cumbrous garments soaking in th' iron "WARSH KITTLE", both ca.: 1890.

The ca.: 1870 APPLEBUTTER STIRRER was to blend and prevent apples sticking when cooked in a big kettle, preferably copper where the fruit would not darken. Materials as iron, especially a nail, spoiled the flavor and could ruin a batch. So when a tightly fit handle loosened a small wooden pin was wedged in. Holes bored in the wood's flat surface made stirring easier by allowing the saucing mixture to slip through. When heat became intense using this 5 ft. mixer others with longer handles were available. During indoors fireplace cookery one with a handle 9 ft. long could be propped through a window. Standing comfortably outside the cook pushed the sauce back and forth in the indoors kettle.

This SOAP STICK (LYE PADDLE) combined strong-smelling cooking grease saved from fat meat scraps with lyes made from fireplace ashes . . . "best done in the dark of the moon". Its auger drilled holes made stirring the cooking mess easier and alkalines have bleached it white. Cut up raw potatoes added to the saved fats helped keep them from becoming rancid. 1790.

If soft soap was preferred over hard chunks, SOAP GOURDS could be used. With their tops sliced off and retained as lids to preserve moisture, seeds and pulp scraped out, and the shells sundried, these big Gourds have been so used for generations. Newly cooked soap poured in and allowed to "set" was then scooped out as needed with long-handled wooden paddles and spoons, these latter preferably handcut from sassafras if available since that wood imparted a better odor to the soap. Plantation raised.

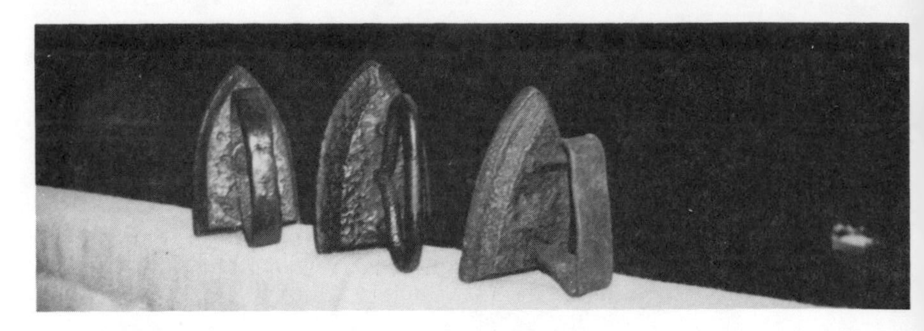

SADIRONS "never to be used for hammering nails or cracking nuts" have each had a Smithy's forging touch. Left is the oldest with its wide handle attached at center in a pretty iron rosette. Right had the handle originally attached at the early 1-spot center, finally burned off and replaced with a handle forged on in two places. ca.: 1850s. The middle handle is reversed; it is the youngest with evident bumps where its first handle was twice-held, then replaced at center. ca.: later 1800s.

Some people used a cold iron late in the past century for smoothing linen washables in the belief that heat deteriorated and yellowed the fabric although heat was more generally used.

A small pine FOOTSTOOL with wide sides and bracket feet holds a heavy polished-golden brass CANDLESTICK ca.: 1840 10" high and one of the glazed pale yellow MILK PITCHERS with brown cows on two sides and greentoned trim . . . cows on anything much sought after in the original by collectors . . . this from the 1800s and now reproduced, although the copies look like copies, the colors too-bright and the animals not too well formed.

The left hatcheled (combed) FLAX was spun into coarse thread (cord). The right completed linen CORD was handtied to form the NETTING. These examples were found in a Pennsylvania Amish country storage building closed almost a hundred years.

A handcarved maple FLAX HATCHEL has holes at either end for hanging. The sharply pointed iron spikes are customarily (as here) driven through metal which is then fastened to the wood backing. The flax was pulled through the teeth.

The large handcut HATCHEL made and used since the mid-1800s by the Amish has oversized iron teeth fastened to the wood by a wide iron band; it has iron rings at the sides and widest top for anchoring to keep it rigid when in use.

WOOL CARDERS set thickly with brad-type wire teeth forced through a thin sheet of leather nailed to maplewood were 1800s handmade in upper New York State, the reverse side slotted for the insertion of removable wooden handles. The pair pulled oppositely to fluff and more evenly mix raw wool first washed (which removed natural oils), then larded to replace those oils. Next a reverse action stripped out the resultant sliver of wool, this sliver ready to be spun into coarse yarn. Women could do this carding seated at a table.

If today's scarcity is any indicator this black enameled iron BUGGYWHIP HOLDER was shop made in limited quantities; Pat. dated Sep 1889-1899 it hung from the high ceiling of a New Hampshire Country Store on a long wire hook displaying even longer Buggywhips. Here it swings from a barn HORSECOLLAR HOOK.

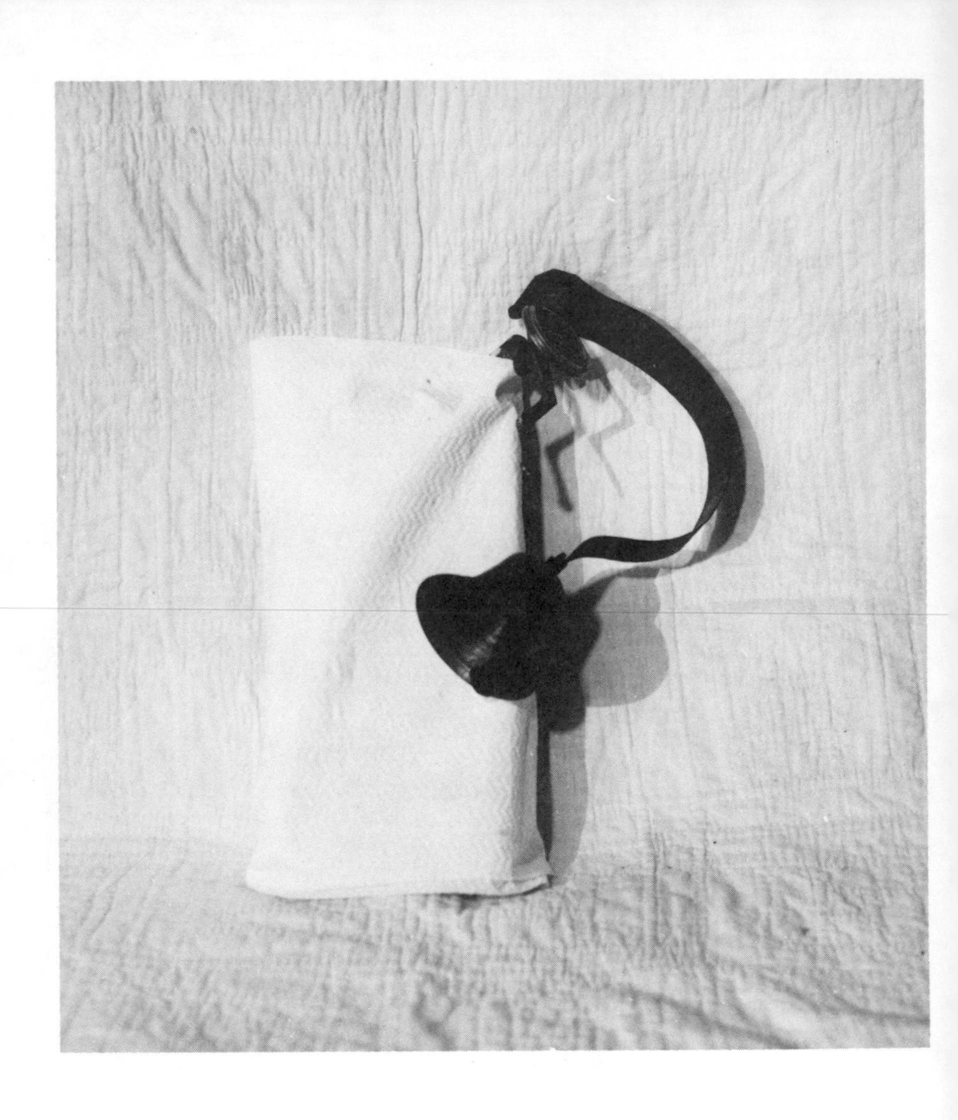

This mid-1800s brass SHOPBELL and clapper on an iron spring with a pretty brass flower at the end of a long iron spike for mounting above the door in a shop was just as typical in the 1600s. When the top of the opening door touched it, the Bell musically vibrated back and forth, announcing incomers to the proprietor. In the late 1800s Mary Ann Gogin was the first woman to manage a General Merchandising Store on the main street of Palestine, Illinois. We are told she sold everything from a box of candles to chicory for flavoring and extending coffee . . . and today in the town a plaque is her affectionate tribute.

Hung outside a JEWELER'S STORE advertising his wares in the mid to latter 1800s was this iron POCKET WATCH. Especially in the smaller towns this merchant-craftsman then also repaired clocks and watches just as many still do today, usually pasting a signed and dated repair tag on the back . . . many of which are still on clocks today. Here the paint has perhaps been retouched but it is skillfully done to the original. These interesting and attractive old TRADE SIGNS are in great demand and not inexpensive. (Abercrombie).

A plaster BONNET MOLD from a Ladies' Bonnet Shop long ago in New England has dried yellowish traces of the original fish glues used in pressing on and shaping the frames.

An iron BREAD PAN with pretty designs around the wide flat edge may have been used in a pastry shop of the mid-1850s, the center lines impressed into the top of baked loaves. Different.

The crop was Cotton . . . the Factors were Commission Merchants . . . the terms Make Liberal Advances on Cotton the method of commitment for anticipated crop acreage yields.

Beyond nostalgia . . . and the uncertainties of historical forevers . . . a faded heavy rolled sheet tin ADVERTISING SIGN describes in a few words whole generations of regional living unlike anywhere else in the world . . . our American Southland . . . ending in 1865 . . . yet still influencing present trade practices.

Wooden SHIPPING BOXES were in use for about a hundred years. This one from the mid-1700s was kept on the counter or floor of a General Emporium, the powder taken out with a scoop for soapmaking. (But if you touched it with damp hands it'd like t' lif' th' hide clean off'n y'). When ordinary store-bought soap eventually became available it could be carefully extended at home. First sliced and dissolved in boiling water, salsoda, borax, and cold water added, it was then allowed to set (congeal). Powdered resin was stirred in for hard yellow soap. However, most folks continued making their own from scratch.

An iron FISHTAIL SCALE (a type popular with Collectors) complete with weights and a brass weighing arm and brass screws releasing the top iron plate was factory stamped at the Howe Scale Company, Rutland, Vermont in the last century. Good red paint holds on after daily usage in a rural mill handling small purchases of flour and meal.

This solid brass WINCHESTER MEASURE is one of a very limited number made during the last century by the Howe Scale Co. of Vermont and as here (and marked) "Patd Dec 18, 1877" on the arm, "WINCHESTER BUSHEL" on the sliding arm weight, and "E & T FAIRBANKS & CO, St. JOHNSBURY, VT.", these used well into the 1900s. Suspended by the large ring seen at the front with the Pail filled it operated in a manner similar to the old Steelyards; in a southern Illinois prairie granary it helped determine moisture content and yield per acre of various grains.

(Prior to 1650 the market town of Winchester, England approved a system of standard weights and measures as pts., qts., pecks, bushels, etc. recognized in America. The weights set by the U.S. Government, as for potatoes, barley, oats, corn, and so on might vary from item to item and in some cases even from state to state.)

A 20" diameter 28" high BUTCHERIN' BLOCK about 1840 found in the midwest is sycamore wood with strong debarked sapling legs. Its first-smooth top is now covered with shallow knife and cleaver marks. As trees grow in less than perfect rounds so is this 9" thick solid slab. The sides carry traces of "coffin red" original paint.

From its size it was probably used in a small crossroads store or kept handy right at the farm.

Much sought after today these are just as useful but more decoratively regarded than when they were first made, having come a long way from the Butcherin' Shed to the home.

Regionally a DUTCH CROWN in the Great Lakes area this early 1800s smithy-made MEAT RACK held large slabs of bacon and hams for slicing or even quarters of fresh meat ready to be cut. Today these are being heavily reproduced but without the obvious early handcrafting.

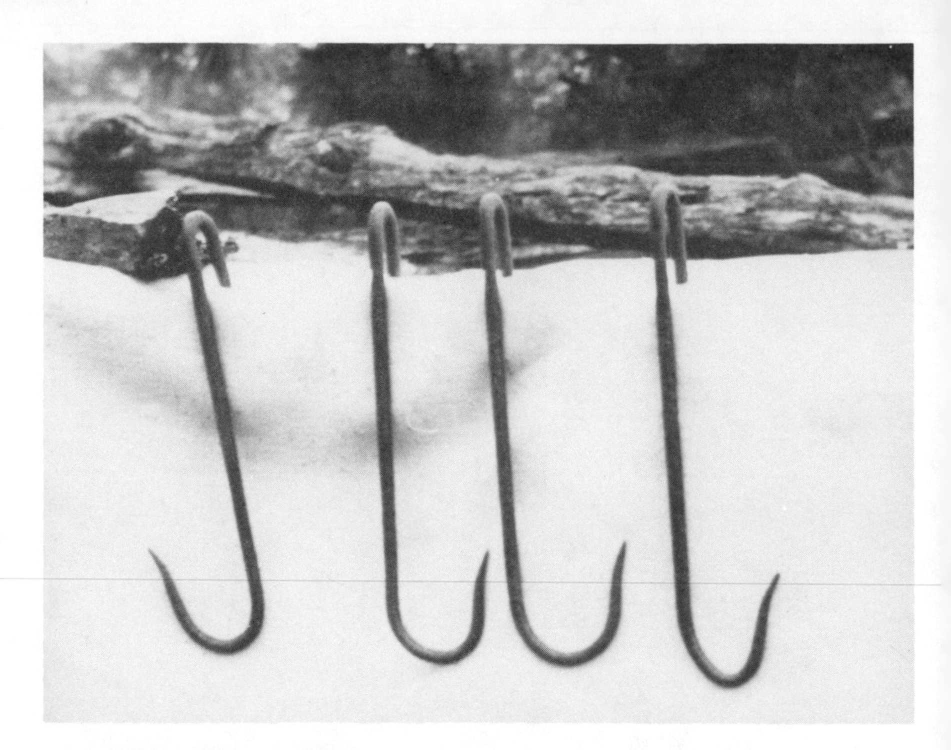

Forged MEATHOOKS in the 1800s were often riveted to a board. In small Butcher Shops which usually had cedar shavings deep on the floor these Hooks held hams and other cured meats in view of the shoppers.

The Cobbler in his shop kept maple SHOELASTS in all sizes, sometimes grouped to the individual shoe and boot needs of an entire family. In use they fit on a metal rod with the sole upright. Iron shoelasts were more commonly found in homes where father or grandpa made the repairs. 1800s-1890s.

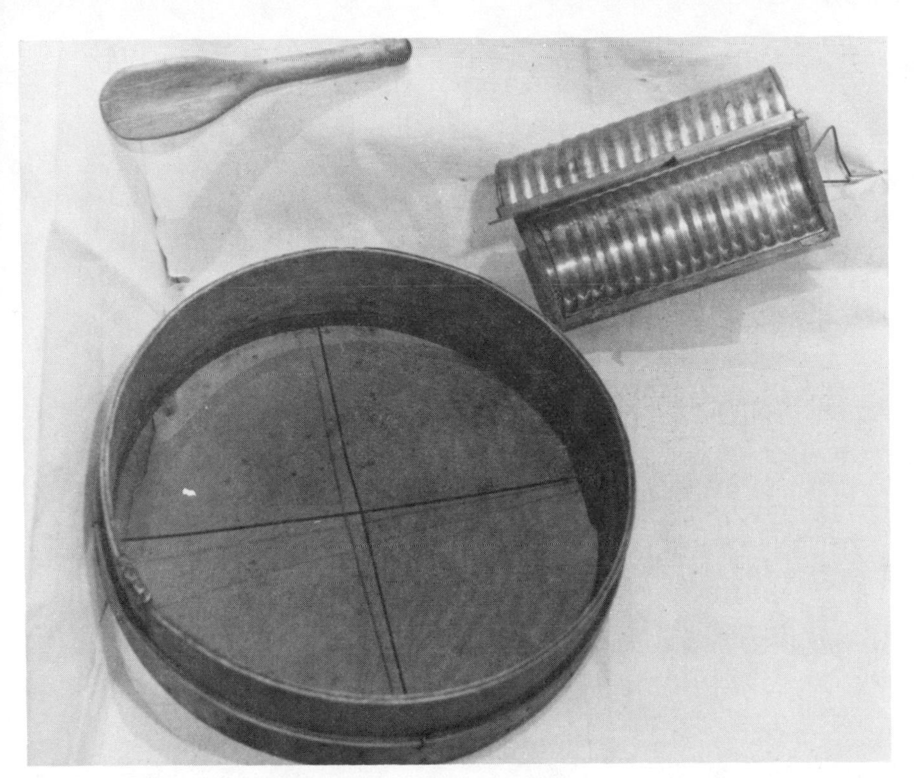

A baker used this wire screened SIFTER to shake lumps out of his flour which came in barrels. The tin BREAD PAN has transparent mica (isinglass) at one end to observe browning. It was ridged to more evenly cut slices of baked white bread. The earlier STIRRING SPOON has a hump cut straight across its thick back to scrape the sides of the kettles and thus could be laid flat on a table without tipping. ca.: 1800s.

Progress of the cotton mills in the 1880s gradually decreased cabin spinning and weaving. These hard dogwood SHUTTLES used at the mills have brass fittings with soft wool pads on both sides of the center posts to protect the flying threads. Now replaced with plastics, many of the original Shuttles were burned but enough remain to warrant seeking.

An 8" long alligator-like tool known as a CORK PRESS, beautifully detailed, was bolted to the counter of an Apothecary Shop well over a hundred and thirty years ago.

A closest-to-desired-size cork slightly dampened and laid in one of the four top and bottom matched ridged spaces was compressed to better fit by bringing down the top lever, squeezing the cork. Inserted in a medicinal jar or bottle it expanded to seal the contents.

These must have been extensively used for many were the corks pushed down in disgust (and pieces) when they resisted the corkscrew . . . and digging with a table fork.

Cough syrup was inevitably taken "WITH CORK" as long as it lasted!

A burnished tinned iron CANTEEN with its strong iron bail is thought to have swung from a hook in a CSA medical fieldwagon 1861-1865 carrying drinking water to the wounded.

The round brass SIEVE with its brass mesh was used in an Apothecary's Shop in the latter 1800s and has imprinted the name of its Philadelphia maker.

A heat-blackened iron Apothecary's WARMING & COOKING PAN FOR MEDICINAL BREWS has a worn porcelain lining and a pouring lip. Side handles fit uniquely designed holds with center slots, these being cast as part of the bowl. Although the handles are secure when slipped over these side knobs they will slip off easily. ca.: 1870.

Pat. dated Apr. 1872 this TRAVEL LAMP & STOVE consists of eleven parts; the tin, lid, handle, three supports for the pan held by the brass reservoir base, brass wick holder, snuffer, rod with inside wick and heat release vents, and a cork stopper for leftover alcohol . . . nine of these fit into the tightly lidded pan with its tiny ring bail. Used in home bedrooms and by Field Nurses it was also a traveling convenience for heating milk and could be lightly carried in a satchel.

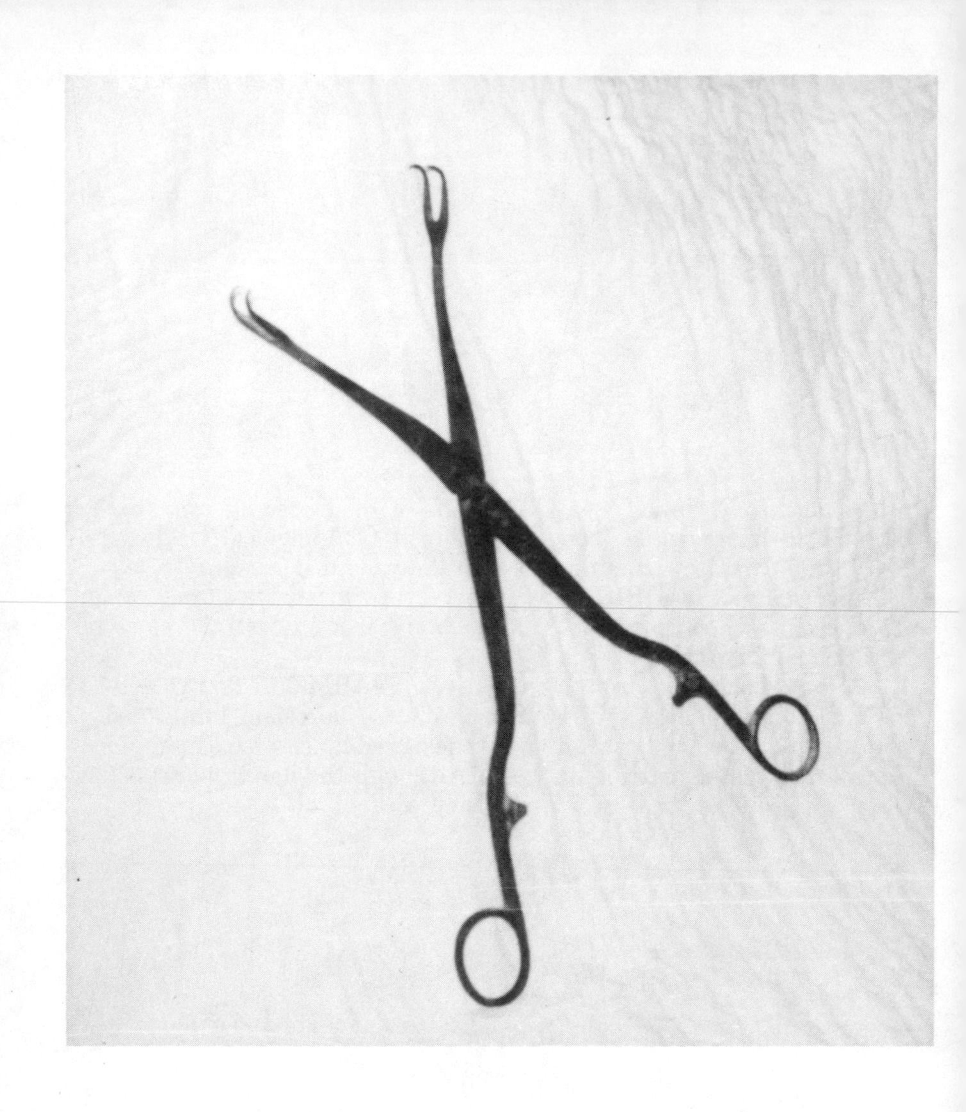

A 1700s discolored wrought iron FORCEPS (Bullet Extractors) with grip-holds and prongs that taper into pinpoint ends; firm for application the two sections, one half-round-slotted fit into the half-exposed rivet at the center hinge of the other, easily slipped apart for carrying in a flat case . . . or wiping.

The very sharp blades of this late 1700s discolored unsterile FLEAM fold into the middle of the brass double handle at right. Used with a pewter or brass basin curved to fit against the body this early bloodletter "beneficially" pilfered about a pint from an arm vein for almost every illness, the amount of blood taken proportioned to the severity of the disease. Thus the gravely weakened patient fought not only the sickness but the cure.

TALLOW mixed with TURPENTINE was a rousing but effective treatment for cleansing and healing gashes while laid-on rags dipped in and wrung out of boiling water were unwitting germicides.

Southern grown perennial PECONIA PLANTS had moisture in their wet-like stems said to coagulate blood on cuts, the seeds popular food flavorings. But a handful of COBWEBS held tightly to a wound was a more universal clotting agent . . . and every cabin had some.

Rubbed on warts the caustic poisonous to taste bright orange juice from the heart-shaped leaves (resembling bloodroot) and stems of PLUME POPPIES was considered a removal remedy for warts. More welcome, however uncertain, were favorite Grandpas who at a mysterious time on the right Almanac Day (fully consulted) could remove warts by massaging with a copper penny taken from their small leather drawstring coinbags, muttering meanwhile queer secret words and raising the penny to pass it around in the air in ways known only to them . . . a ritual that could be imparted to a woman by a man, to a man by that woman, never in the same family. And each so accorded this accolade could pass it along to only one other person.

A daub of mud or a chaw of moist chewed-up plug or loose-pouch tobacco was a soothing drawing poultice for wasp, bee, and hornet stings.

Sulphur and molasses that "y' tuk t' do y' good" might have been a fine spring blood purifier but stewed rhubarb tasted better . . . and went down a whole lot easier.

Grandmothers were usually strong advocates of camphorated oil dripped over lard already knife-spread on a piece of flannel . . . the whole "rimidy" over-warmed . . . overnight on the throat and/or chest it got rid of the soreness, the idea being that the grease went through the skin "an' got at th' roots".

And every family had its passel of favorite "receipts" it obligingly shared with (foisted on) everybody else . . . for just about everything . . . real or imagined!

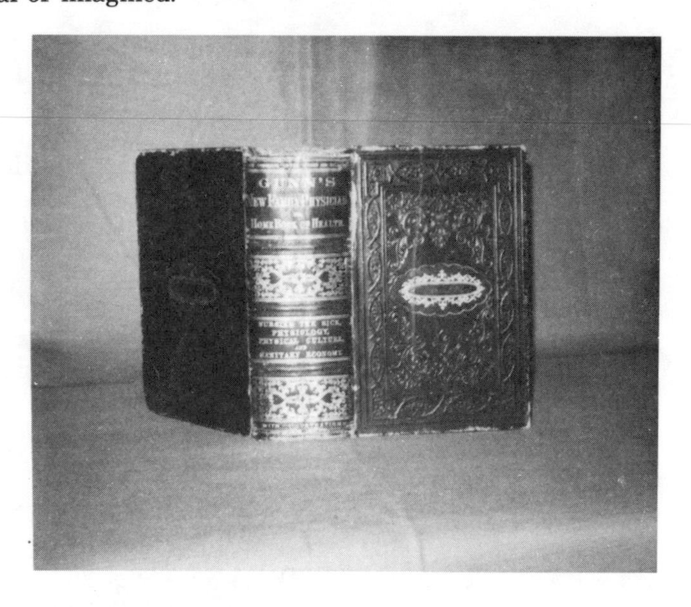

One helpful panacea toward soothing the anxieties of self-dependency in early cabin and later rural care of the sick and injured, and the worrisome uncertainties of dosing and poulticing with natural concoctions, was this goldtooled leatherbacked 1887 revised edition of GUNN'S NEW FAMILY PHYSICIAN or HOME BOOK OF HEALTH first issued in 1857. It soon became essential for every bride who could obtain one . . . and along with health care gave dozens of receipes for a variety of things as catsup and whitewash. (My Grandma was a believer.)

Another book published a short time later suggested that in the event of chimney fires (frequently occurring if the inside bricks were not regularly cleared of soot) . . . "ascend to the roof and throw salt down the chimney".

Tinnermade around 1850 is a DOCUMENT CARRIER to hold maps, medical papers of Field Surgeons, homesteading surveys and deeds, and sermons for circuit-riding preachers when space was at a premium, fitting nicely into saddlebags. Few were made. During the Civil War Officers sometimes bought them for preserving Commission papers and carrying field orders. When shopmade they were usually of japanned tin while the tinnermade were plain metal.

An American tin TEA CADDY ca.: 1820-1830 has its original tole type green paint, now faded. A conch shell design is on the front, a deep lid has a white china knob, and two inside compartments held separate kinds of tea. (Tea leaves were first shipped from China to ports in Holland soon after 1600; by 1650 the fragrant brew was being popularly steeped throughout Europe and England, thence to America.)

The owner of this shoe-foot stretcher-base TILTTOP TAVERN TABLE from c: 1810 suggests it was made from black oak. (Abercrombie).

All original Tavern Tables as this of good quality are very popular today but it takes a bit of time and patience to find one, and well worth the searching.

Progressing from earlier tin and pottery an imaginative American Pewterer created this TEA JAR from what appears to be a type of black quartz adding a Pewter Lid. Oddly, it is pitted with shallow nicks I can't explain other than to suppose it might have long stood on the back of a shelf with heavier storage being carelessly shoved against its sides; one of those pieces we buy simply because we like them. ca.: 1890.

Interesting to display alone or combined with wood or even iron collectibles are these imprinted glazed stoneware WHOLESALERS' JUGS from the last century.

Each has its own description . . . the top middle has the year "1883" embossed across the darker front top.

The lower left might be a little earlier according to its shape; it evidently was made to a particular customer's order since it mentions the name and business of the Proprietor.

Lower right "Augusts" has a wider mouth with a slight pouring lip so it was probably a pouring Pitcher-Jug.

A 30" high 26" diameter COPPER BARREL from a New England Distillery has two iron handles, a few unavoidable dents, and is of about 40 gallons capacity. 1880

A pine TRUNK owner marked on the brass lid plate, the iron strap frame showing evidence of individual handcrafting, perhaps the nearest blacksmith. It has brass studs, a tin patch, and an iron hasp rather than the more common keyhole padlock. c 1870.

Owner-initialed about 1850 this handsome square TRAVEL BOX (also called a BACHELORS' BOX) is of light tan leather covered wood with an iron lock and key. Iron strap bands are held with big brass studs. Inside is a patterned paper liner with webbed cotton strips for keeping tall bottles and such upright. The flowered top tray comes down with a leather pull to reveal a narrow space for flat-packing under the lid. Plantation.

A man on either handle of these massive LOG TONGS could lift, easily flip over due to wing tangs added by the smithy, and carry the wooden ties (sleepers) to a roadbed where steel tracks were fastened with iron spikes, the spikes usually dated to determine age of the ties for replacement.

The FORMING AXE has its original woodenhandle.

Both RAILROAD TOOLS were fashioned by a latter 1800s smithy employed by a particular "line", this a common custom among the railroads.

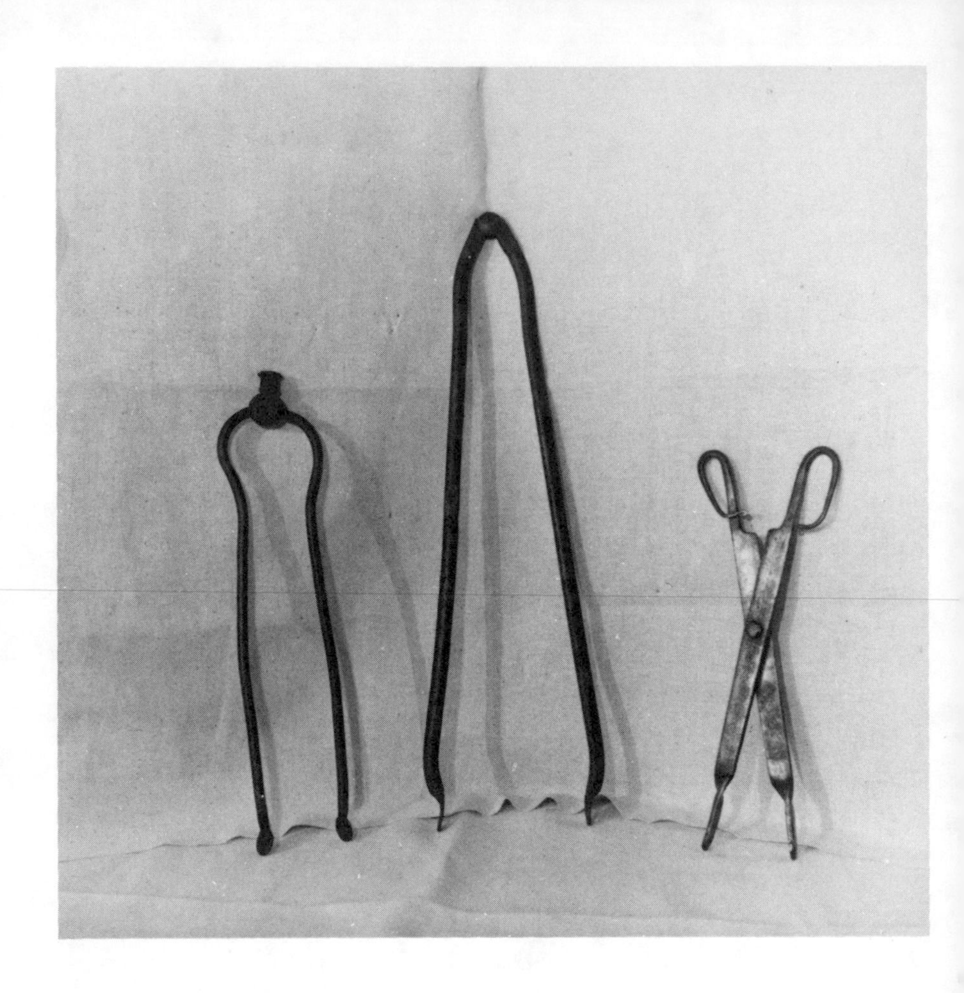

Finely handfashioned are these from a late 1700s settlement: rat-tail top swirls on SMOKING (EMBERS) TONGS that carried coals from the hearth up to tobacco tamped in long-handled clay pipes kept in a wallbox at fireside; uneven FIRE TONGS at left and the last made from BUGGY BRACES.

Cast in sand iron CARRIAGE STEPS with grooved edges and center diamond design meant to attractively roughen the tread-tops were bolted one at either side of a vehicle about 1840. Placed at an angle to further avoid foot slippage they dipped low to the ground as the coach springs depressed under weight on the steps. Swaying over dusty roads these might have carried th' womenfolks "spendin' " (vistitin') or th' whole family t' town.

Three FORGE SHOVELS carried coals to and ashes from the blacksmith's forge, extra care used in fashioning the right. The heavier front POKER could also have been found in homes to loosen fireplace coals. The slim FLUE RAKE cleared soot and other stoppages from later kitchen and parlor stovepipes. 1870.

L. to R. . . . blacksmith's SOFTNOSED PUNCH and a SET HAMMER, both forged, the latter with the original handle; farrier's SHOEING HAMMER and carpenter's BRAD or TACK HAMMER. Late 1800s.

The long spikey NAILS were leftovers from an early Kentucky covered bridge.

Two factory iron SHOES had the customary reshaping from the farrier. Kept loose in empty nail kegs around the forge, grouped to types and sizes (if he was a tidy shopkeeper), one was chosen nearest an animal's requirements and held with tongs, heated red hot, hammered on the anvil, and fitted before being nailed onto the hoof. 1890 (Shoes must always be nailed onto a wall with open side up so one's luck doesn't run out.)

This oak SHOEIN' RACK from the 1780s had three boards cut and fit as cleverly as a puzzle. Mostly a farrier just put the hoof between his knees readying it for shoeing and throughout the procedure but with an excitable or just plainly mean animal he laid the foot in such a simple rack, thus gaining more freedom to work.

CURRY COMBS had many variations but were principally rows of thin dull-edged teeth with some sort of handle. The farrier held the comb in one hand to curry the animal's coarse hair and followed his strokes brushing down the hair with his other hand . . . or with a cloth or a brush. In barns, town Livery Stables . . . wherever there were horses . . . there were Combs.

This HOOF KNIFE marked "E.J. POPE 1889" with one sharpsided thin blade bent over at the end was a "trimmer" to clean out the inside sole of the hoof before a shoe was nailed on.

A horse attracted a nagging swarm of flies with foremost th' consarned big horseflies, worse if he had to stand still. They made him shie nervously or even kick the farrier while being shod. So an apprentice, the animal's owner, or even the farrier himself kept after the pests with this brushing FLYSWITCH contrived from the tail of a deceased horse, the hair still on the hide held by wire wrapped around the stick. Not a sophisticated tool but it worked pretty well. 1860.

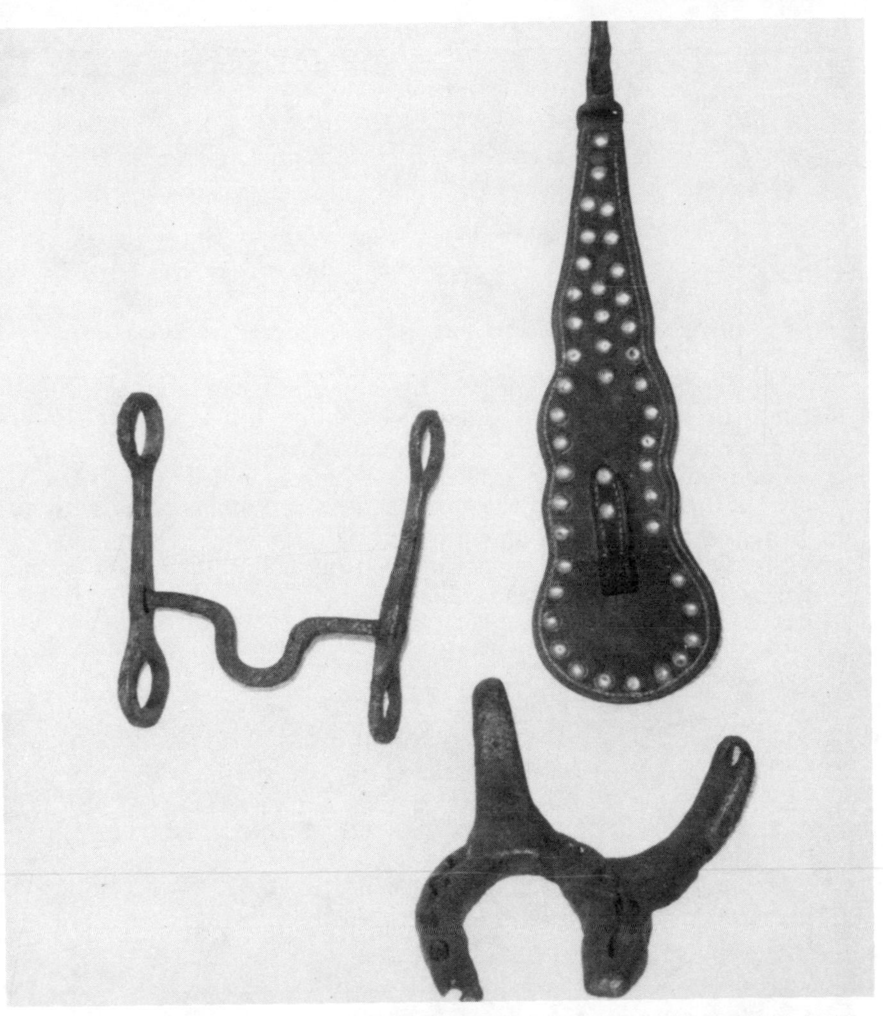

The handforged LONG PORT BRIDLE BIT was placed in the animal's mouth to curb (restrain) him; the double thickness stitched leather brass studded KIDNEY DROP was a pad for that portion of the body against the pull of the reins; to this unique and rare orthopedic PONY TRAINING SHOE the farrier added heavy iron guides to throw the foot into a straight-ahead gait.

The feet of horses, mules and oxen were not all identical and just as we must have our shoes individually fitted, so did they, many having foot problems needing a special shoe adjustment which a good farrier was trained to do.

It is generally agreed by researchers that some type of foot covering for horses and bullocks dates back to their earliest domestication. Materials were according to availability and man's resourcefulness, progressing from rushes, skins and cloth to the present iron.

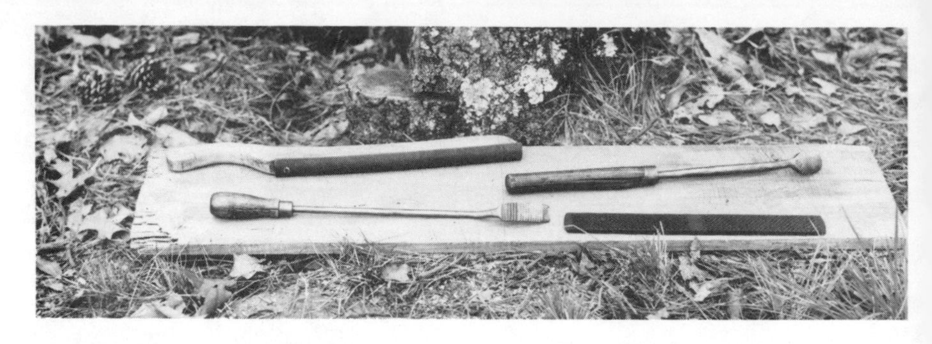

Two farriers' HOOF RASPS - the upper left has teeth set in one diagonal direction with a wood handle extending full length - the lower right has a center division for ridges going oppositely. They file or cut down and smooth the hoof wall before a shoe is added. The FLOATS (Horse Tooth Rasps) filed the sharp edges from molars, and with no parts to hurt the mouth, were not too uncomfortable. The lower left is a two-directional RASP. The upper left was blacksmith made 1800s, the rest were factory made latter 1800s.

At left a hindleg PIGCATCHER has a branch handle and rope eye; lower right is an interesting standard-handle-eye ROOT CUTTER. The front hinged end SHOE PEG FILE smoothed down wooden pegs (usually chestnut) in soles of early boots and shoes, found both with the cobbler and at home. Smithy's tools include l. to r. SPECIAL PURPOSE, STRAIGHT LIP, HOOP TONGS and PINCERS. 1890-95.

Now outmoded each BUTTERIS was forged to the smithy's ideas on a general principle, pressure from the shoulder and chest making less strain on the wrist than using the hoof knife alone. It trimmed the hooves before shoes were put on. Every farrier did not have a "Butt'ris" for it required a special skill to apply. Some craftsmen had neither the natural technique nor the wish to learn. 1800s.

A most unusual thinly rolled sheet iron TRAVELER has a twisted handle with a hanging loop. One of the side indentations is surely intentional for counting the revolutions in measuring but with evident wear in such an early tool . . . which is which? Blacksmith fashioned.

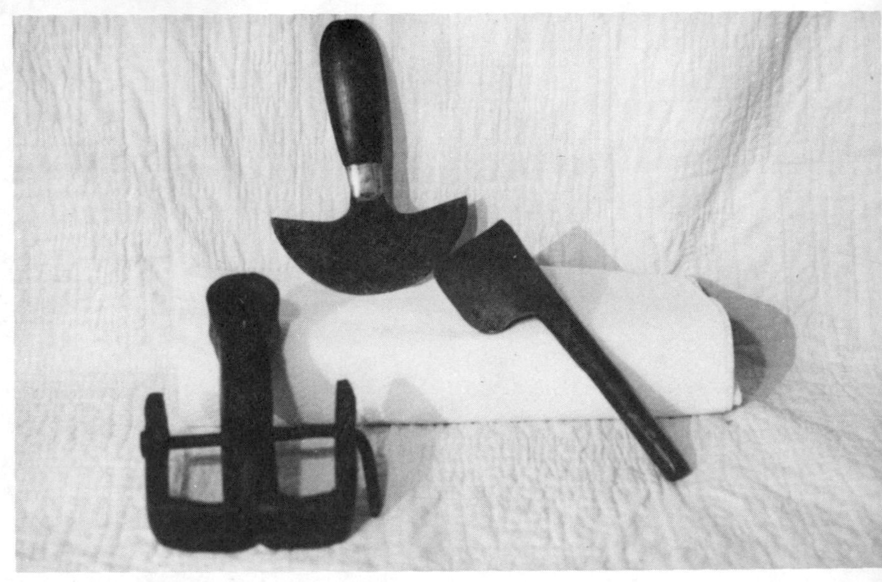

At center a sharp HARNESSMAKER'S KNIFE touches a CLINCH CUTTER, or as an ex-smithy termed it, a BRADDER. Often made from a rasp, this farrier used one iron piece, folding it to also form the handle. The tool's blunt top shows evidence of hammer blows when the keener lower side was placed under clinched nails to straighten them out prior to a horseshoe being pulled off with nippers. The left CONJECTURABLE, possibly related to a CLEVIS, was artfully forged a long time ago, one heavy iron bar bent at middle to form an eye, the ends pulled down parallel and then oppositely turned with eye ends to accommodate a long spike.

With a TRAVELER (Tracing Wheel) he had forged with a loop for hanging one 1700s smithy first measured the outside rim of a wooden wheel either he or a wheelwright had made. Next he measured the length of the iron rim (tire) he must form to fit the wheel. This Follower has none of the numbers later stamped to count revolutions of the wheel. Instead we see only a small outer edge nick for this craftsman had an experienced eye.

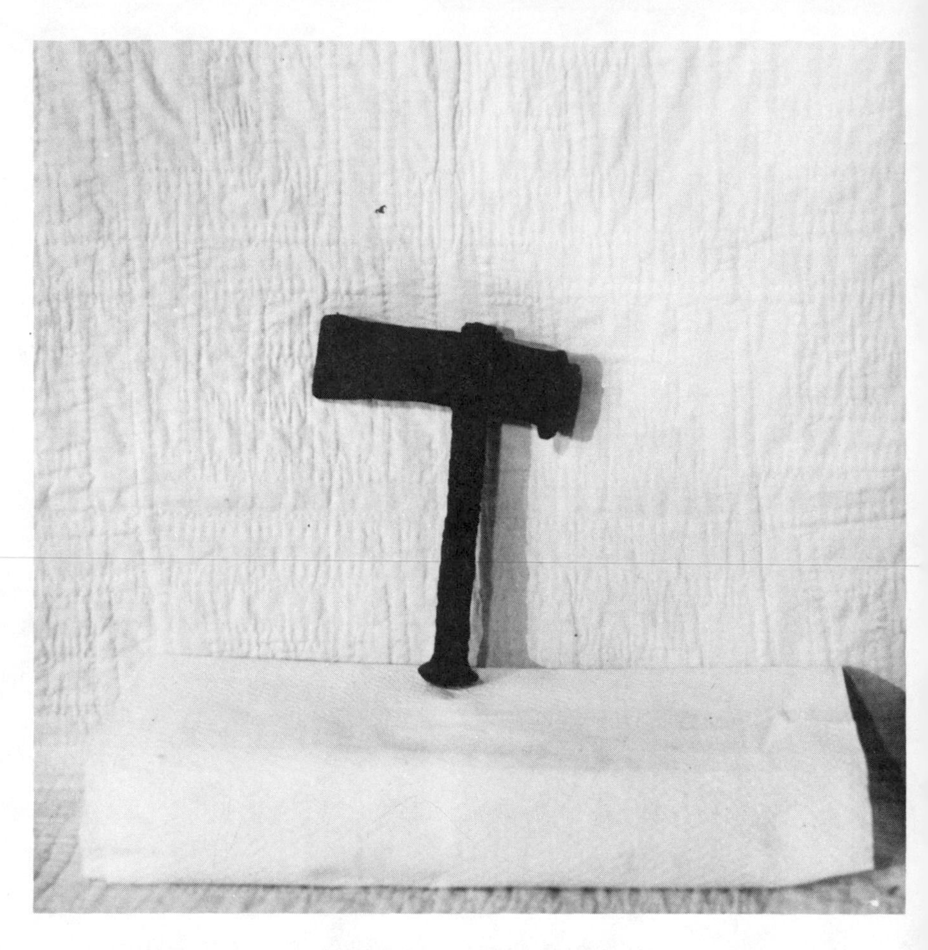

New England SNOWHAMMER (Yankee Snowknocker) about 1810. In the snowbelt regions these followed a general theme but were made in various sizes to order or at the inclination of the smithy. This small one carried handle down on sledges and wagons permitted teamsters to remove caked ice and snow from the tender underside of the horse's foot inside the shoe rim, an impaction that could grow painful or cause him to slip and fall even if equipped with ice calks. Originally having a sharper point, the blunt-small-knob end was used to loosen by tapping the hard ball and the other sharper end was the pick, the whole now encrusted with age, wear, and exposure.

Wherever possible merchants delayed shipping goods until there was enough snow on the ground to use the big horse-drawn sledges whose runners slipped more easily over frozen rough ground than did wagon wheels. And in the late 1800s through the turn of the century snow was hauled, dumped and rolled smooth to cover floorboards of covered bridges, these same rollers later used on plowed ground ready for planting.

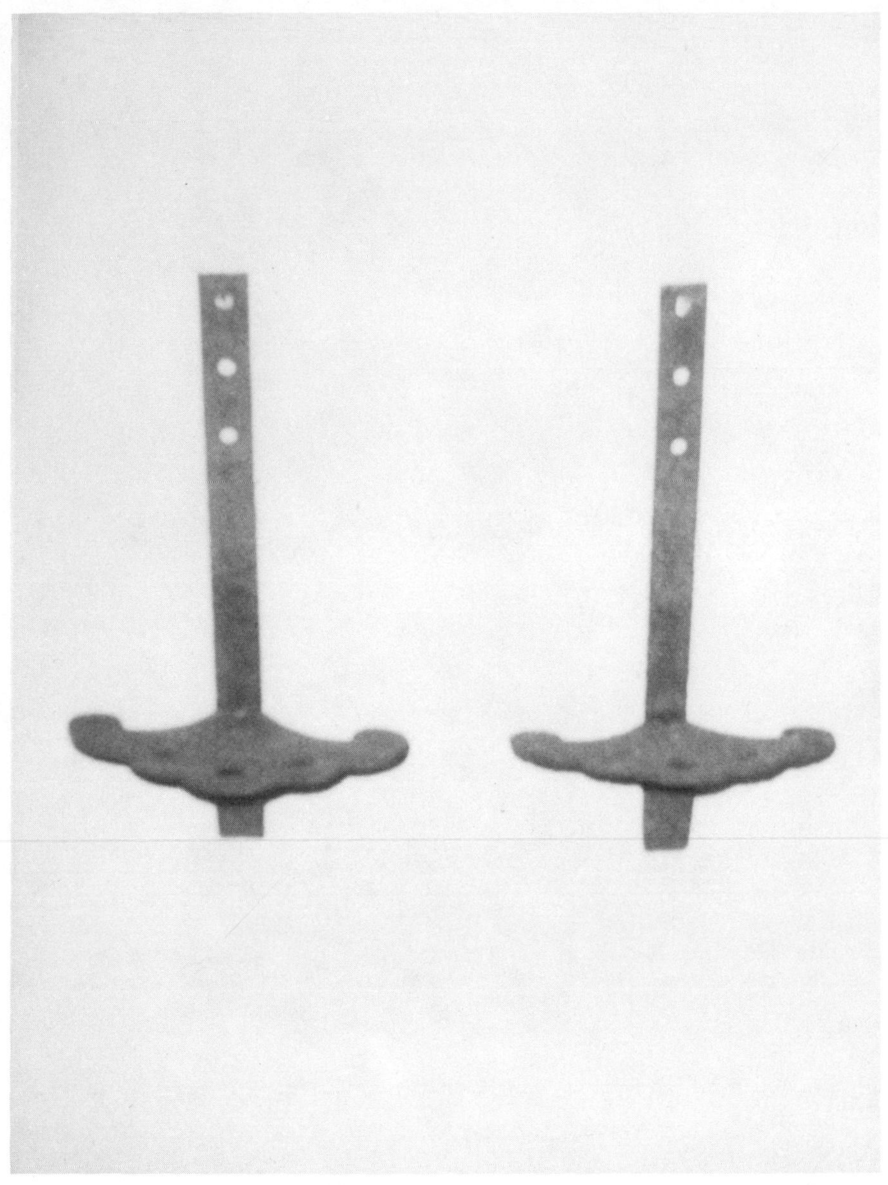

Cast iron plates of many designs on iron straps are regional SNOWBIRDS from the 1800s.

Anchored by the holes to roof edges under materials as slate or tile they were meant to retain snow for insulation.

Others believed they could prevent any layer of snow from plunging down on the heads of pedestrians.

The name occurred because platforms were often shaped like eagles and looking up folks mistook them for feathered perchers.

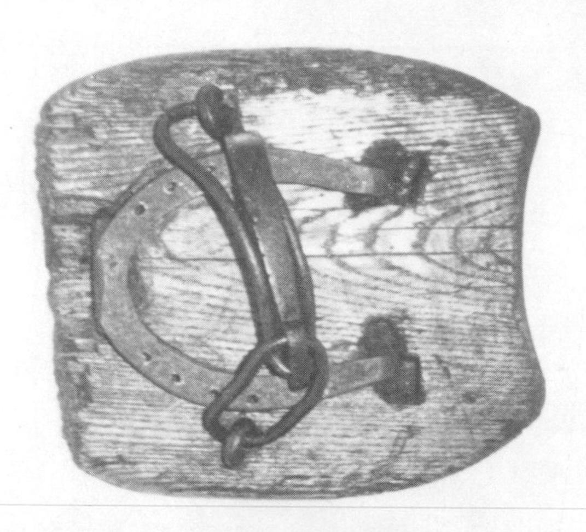

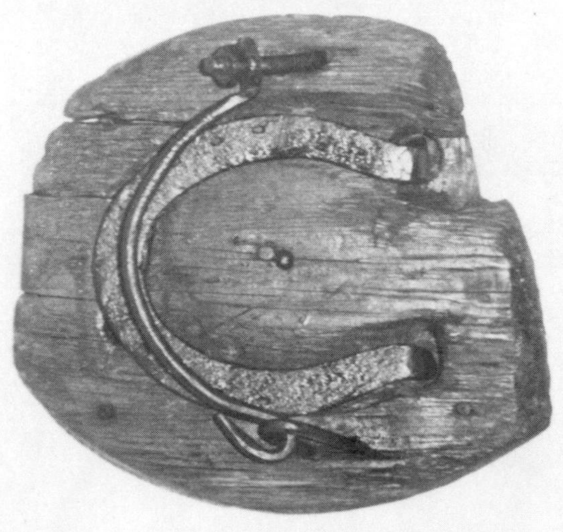

Long out of usage these wooden MUD SHOES kept a horse from sinking deep in muck. On the principle of our snowshoes (walking on top of the snow) the iron pullover clamp or simple bar fastened just above the hoof around the fetlock, sometimes made and fitted in the proper season when the animal was being regularly shod. Especially in the Great Lakes and New England States where spongy and swampy ground made early plowing difficult workhorses so shod could carry on. Loggers found them practical in bogs.

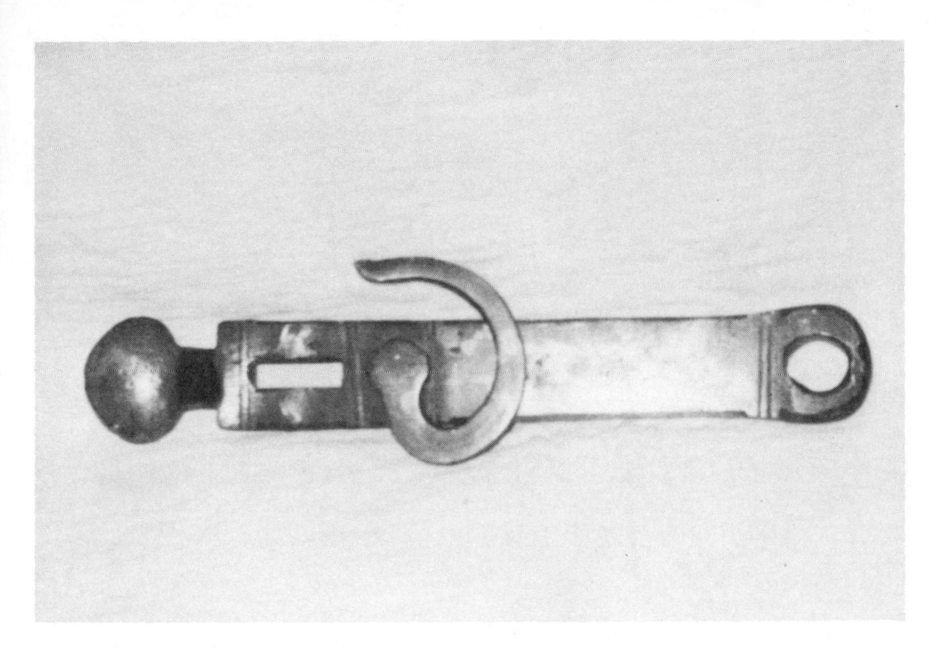

A handsome early 1700s handwrought iron HASP fastened to a door has a riveted swing curve that held fast when the Hasp was placed over a spike or staple. It has been burnished to its original sheen.

A wire basket COAL SAVER could be moved back and forth but is held from slipping off its pole handle by nails bent over at each end. Best known in northern regions it frugally sifted cooled ashes to rescue bits of unburned coal although one family used theirs to shake grease from cracklin's. 1890.

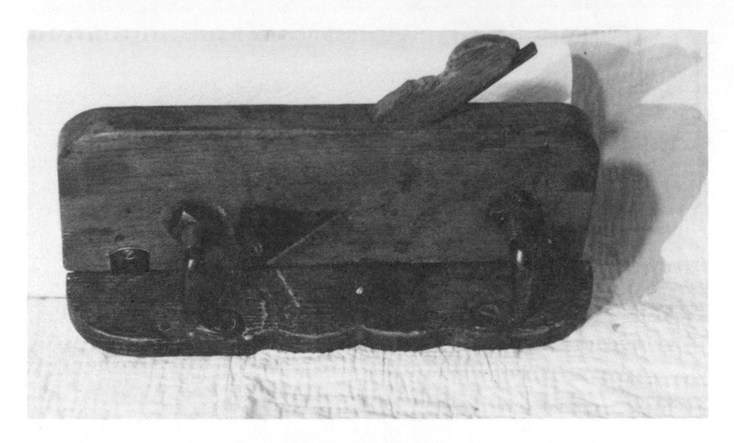

A maple RABBET PLANE about a hundred years old was for cutting a groove in the edge of a board for joining, as a panel. Here the owner added a fancy scallop to a necessary guiding sole.

Initials in a 26" long BIRDSEYE MAPLE TRYING PLANE for smoothing large surfaces as floors designate the owner. When newly formed buds on a maple sapling were unable to push through they appeared as "eyes" when the wood was cut, a quality much in demand a century ago. First sought in trees from far northern hills exposed to steadily-high winds, sleet, rain, and snow that forcibly retarded the young growth, sometime later maples were deliberately planted there for this purpose.

The 33" JOINTING or FLOOR PLANE with its HORN grip fit wood pieces together.

Many railroads, Wells Fargo, and individual craftsmen habitually initialed their tools against theft, losses in lending, and misplacement.

Two among the once-most-widely-used tools are the applewood PLOW PLANE, cutting the groove for which the lower cherrywood TONGUE PLANE cut the tenon, both early 1800s. Each has a fence, the Plow with a side discharge and the Tongue with burl adjusting screws.

It is generally accepted ancient Greece invented the planes . . . or according to specimens found in diggings at Pompeii they could date as far back as around 100 A.D. Smoothing Planes were known in medieval times but these Tongue and Grooving types did not appear until late in the 1600s. Tools whose basic original shapes continue efficiently operable have not changed very much in the last two hundred years and more.

The factory metal MALE TAP on its maple base is half of a pair used to thread holes in which bolts were fitted.

A long cherrywood SLITTING GAUGE with its tiny very sharp blade held by a wood wedge made thin drawer bottoms and such when exact sawing with larger tools was too hard. Mid 1800s.

The SCHNITZLEBANK (SHAVING HORSE) was popular during the 1700s and 1800s mainly because it was a tool on legs "so's y' could set". Many had seat extensions but this made on a base in the 1850s required a stool. The worker's foot on the heavy wooden lever manipulated the upper JAW which clamped tight on barrel hoops, shakes, shingles, and such laid on the slant board, this brought down within easy reach.

This JAW consists of four sections glued and held by an upper wooden and a lower iron bar, this for increased durability, differing from a customary solid wooden block.

The DRAWKNIFE was pulled toward the operator.

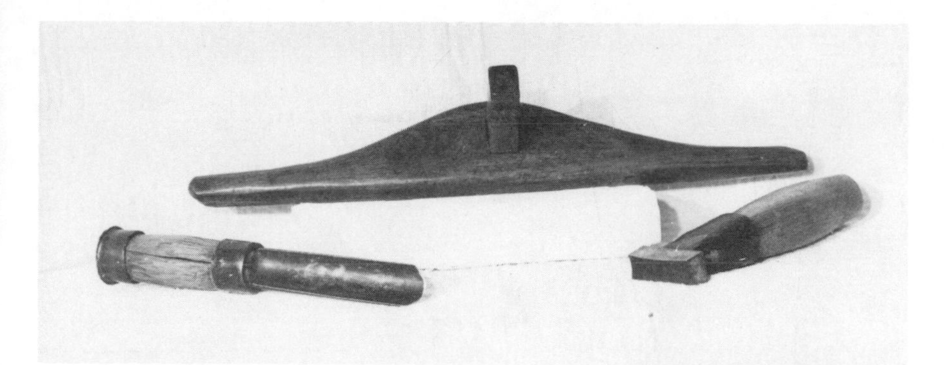

Late 1700s and early 1800s handfashioned COOPERS' TOOLS: an 11" outside-edge-sharpened GOUGE with early type heavy banded handle made curved arcs and holes in wood; the rare cherry SAWTOOTH with its narrow blade was run around the inside top of a barrel marking the line which a Croze blade deepened for fitting in a lid; the initialed HOOP SETTER firmed such things as barrel staves.

Coopers were important personnel on the Mayflower.

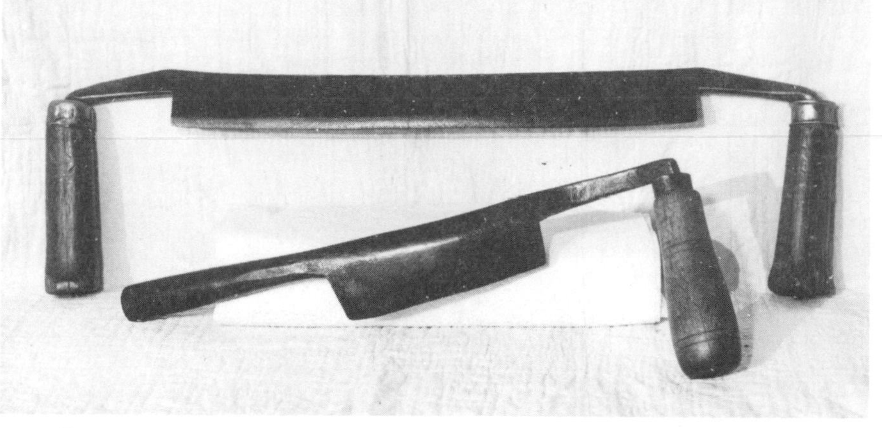

Iron at one end and wood at the other afforded better hand leverage on a COOPER'S CHAMFERING KNIFE (Shaver) that furrowed and beveled wood. Its curved blade folded over on top was not meant for striking.

Among the oldest of the antique tools is the DRAWKNIFE used by woodworkers drawing it to them in a shaving motion. Blades varied in size and shape to usage.

Both early tools were handfashioned with the metal extended into the wood and anchored bent over outside the handle ends. These from 1790-1800.

A small BOWLMAKER'S HAND ADZE for chopping out the unnecessary bulk of wood in making oblong butterbowls, doughtrays, and such, always shaped by hand. 1700s.

From the 1690s a rare blacksmith-made iron WOODWORKING GOUGE (round chisel) 9" long, inside-scoop-edge-sharpened, was for roughing out wood in any circular arc.

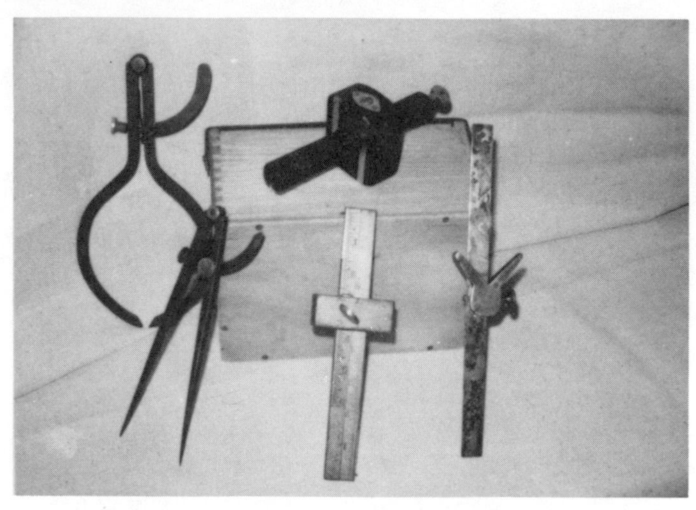

Top l. CALIPERS measured thickness of wood or metal, while DIVIDERS below measured and scribed for all types of woodworkers, both with brass locking screws.

The rare black EBONY MARKING GAUGE top c. with brass inlays dates before 1840, all tools here in that era.

The DOUBLE MARKING GAUGE is uncommon and the r. CENTERING GAUGE has brass RABBIT EARS.

Used mostly by metal workers, this metal CALIPERS also measured wood thickness.

A 23" rosewood PANEL GAUGE (marking) with a holding side wedge measured very wide boards. 1800s.

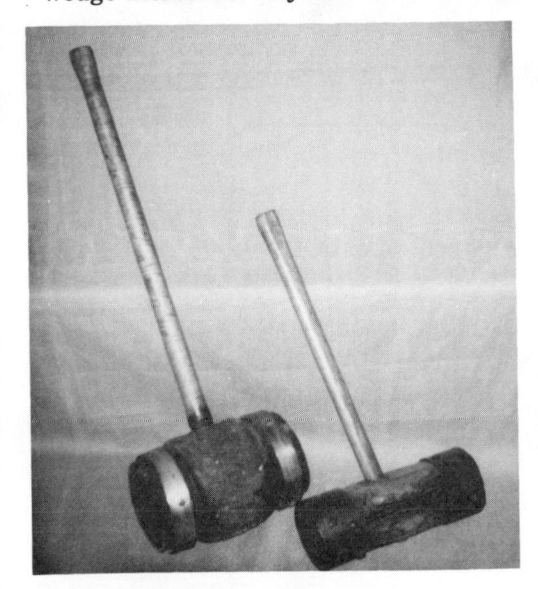

At left an extremely heavy oak SHIP'S MAUL with unusual thick solid brass bands put on by a blacksmith was used to drive huge wedges or anything that needed considerable force. Early.

The smaller but still fairly heavy CIRCUS MAUL has rarely-seen smithy-fashioned heavy iron cups at each end for added weight (strength) and endurance. Although it could be called a Mallet because of its shorter handle, its weight makes it a Maul. mid-1800s.

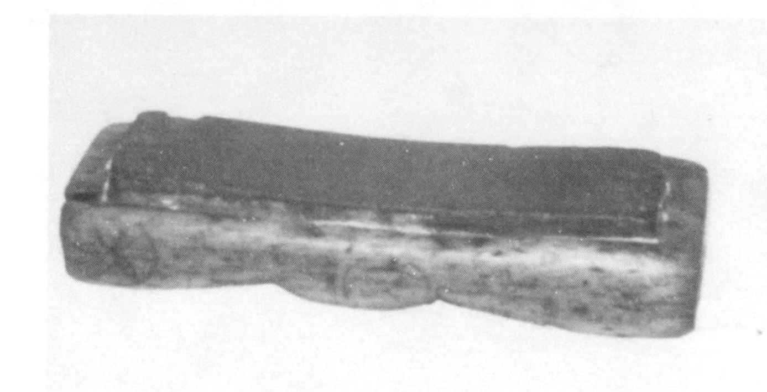

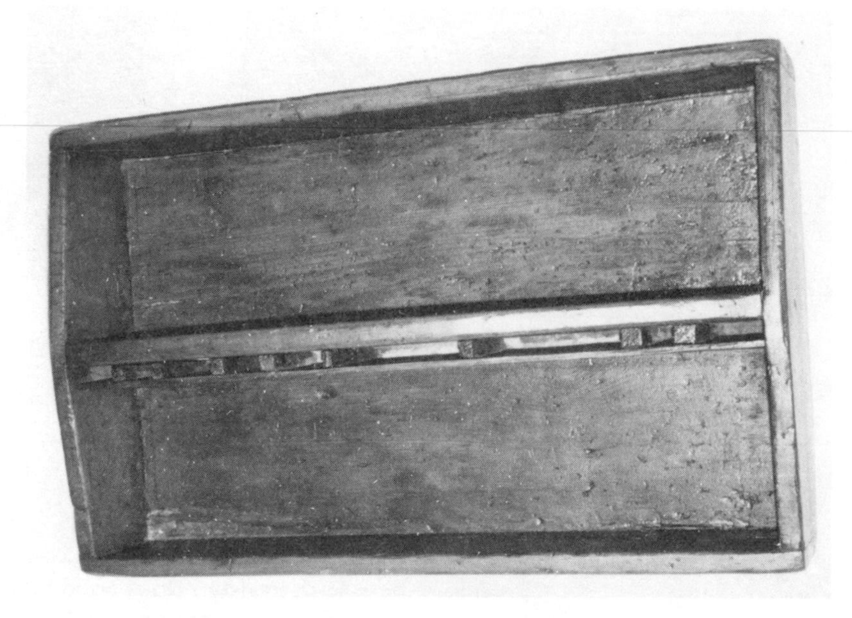

An almost obliterated HEX MARK cut into the side of this pine base 9" OILSTONE (whetstone using oil for sharpening edged tools) shows its Pennsylvania Dutch origin . . . around latter 1700s.

Courting couples of those rural communities created their personal identification sign (to ward off evil), this placed on the Dower Chest the groom-to-be made for the bride-to-be to fill with handiwork and clothing, on their barn, and so on, but not commonly seen on such a tool.

Of countless attractive designs, brightly painted tulips popular, some are truly beautiful.

From the same approximate period and area this CARPENTER'S pine TOOL CARRIER has slots for smaller items.

A cherry Sheraton type STAND about 1820 is woodpegged with a 1-board top 1" thick, 12½" deep and almost 23" in length. Legs with teardrop bases extend to hold the top and a wooden drawerpull becomes its own screw fastener inside the dovetailed drawer.

Found near Bell Witch, Tennessee legend has it that a Bell family from North Carolina homesteaded a farm just north of the settlement. They were soon so harrassed by a Bell Witch . . . clangs, pealing, and so on that even a daughter's suitor was frightened away.

Intrigued by the mystery when he learned of it, Andrew Jackson drove up from Nashville to investigate. As he approached within several miles of the farm his coach wheels locked. Each time the horses were headed back south away from the place the wheels again properly turned.

After repeated futile attempts to proceed to the homestead Mr. Jackson reluctantly gave up and returned to Nashville.

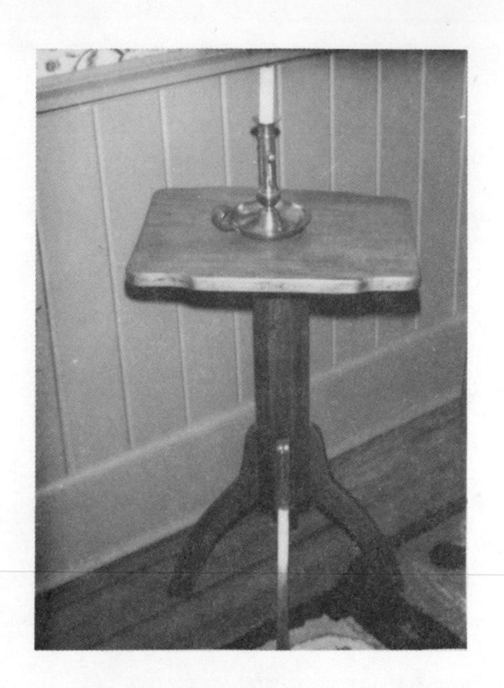

A CANDLESTAND 1840 has an uncommonly larger gumwood top on a cypress pedestal and a 4-leg base. The brass CHAMBERSTICK has a finger bar for easier carrying and a side pushup knob to get every possible inch from the candle's burning with a deep saucer for drippage. These were taken from tables at the foot of stairs and individually carried to bedrooms.

A walnut BLANKET CHEST 31" wide, 27" tall, and 21" deep has opening dovetailing at all four corners and a 1-board top. Brackets have been replaced to the originals. 1840.

Built by a member of the congregation for a 1-room Meetin' House and weekday schoolroom in cotton country this 8 ft. native oak primitive CHURCH PEW has streaks of white buttermilk paint forever imbedded. Still able to serve into a second century, it is surprisingly comfortable, and the unevenly cut arms soften its severity.

Various fiercely-stern Preachers forbade their Flocks to "horsetrade or to go a'wagonin' on the Sabbath unless to and from church . . . an' 'cept fer the Reg'lar Sinners (thet ev'rybuddy knowed who they wuz anyways) . . . the rest of the Faithful so abided."

As it grew older, on a warm night when the moon was down and the scent of the quiet magnolias exuded a temporary serenity, the PEW must have heard a sudden creaking of saddle leather, the abruptly muffled jingle of harness, and the tired snorts of horses as gray or blue cavalry rode cautiously into the churchyard for water and bivouac.

Now almost extinct, unless a few remain on distant country lanes and in the Amish counties, is the HORSE SHED, once part of every church property. They were simple low structures with one side open to shelter animals driven (and tied in the Shed still harnessed to their "rigs") and saddle horses ridden by churchgoers. Some Sheds were wooden, others were caves and prairie sod huts like the barns at the beginning of our 18th century . . . just as Settlers themselves had to "make do" awaiting building of their cabins.

A COVERLET on the ARROWBACK SETTLE 1825 has: "John Wissler Wayne Co. (county) Indiana 1840" while the other (with its raggedy fringe) half inside the domeback wooden mid-1800s TRUNK is dated "1857". Both are double woven wool and linen, wool taking the homemade or store-bought dyes and the resistant linen left natural. The patterns and colors reversed, dark sides being up in winter and light sides being up in summer . . . particularly beautiful ones saved for the bed in the "spare room".

The wall shows how effectively we may decorate with early heritage, including a baker's sifter, stuffed toy cats and dried grasses. Striking is the typically late 1800s picture of Someone's Uncle who must have stiffly sat awhile with his neck in a back vise to keep him motionless for a time exposure. (Jill Wasson).

This WALL GROUPING shows many objects still not difficult to find: DOUGHTRAYS and PANTRY TOOLS, a FARM FEED BOX, HAY RAKE, WASHTUB, HAND COFFEE GRINDER, CABBAGE CUTTER, etc. 1800s; a handcut from one-piece-of-wood GRAIN SHOVEL and a 3-prong HAYFORK 1810-20. Blue on gray design CROCKS 1870 are at the top of a handfashioned open-top 2-solid-drawer-base pine DRESSER c: 1800s. Cupboards of some type were made here beginning soon after 1650 although history first mentions them in the fourteenth century. (Jelly cupboards rarely if ever had locks.) This piece expresses the simple sturdy lines of most rural cabinetmakers who had no access to patterns . . . yet shows a unique appeal as a primitive. (Jill Wasson.)

A handcarved BOX, generally called a Bible Box and greatly used for that purpose, has lunette (half moon) carvings and top flutes. Pine was considerably used although walnut as here was characteristic of Pennsylvania. This dates early in the 1700s and could be 1690s. (Abercrombie).

A mid-1800s FOOTWARMER is tinner-made of rolled sheet iron on a black painted dovetailed wooden frame. Holes punched at top allowed heat to escape from the pre-heated charcoals scooped into the pullout drawer. A wire bail with a wooden handhold and a wide metal rear handle provide easy carrying. Although fireplaces served most rooms at home this Warmer was available, but more often it was taken to church and kept underfoot; sermons were long, churches were cold, and no matter how bundled up they were, folks' feet got cold back then too. Plantation.

A 4-piece handcut partially smoothed pinewood double CANDLESTICK with holders part of the top wings is post self-pegged, fitted below into a round slot at the center of two dovetailed crosspieces. pre-1850. Plantation.

Pre-1848 wrought iron 3½ ft. tall CANDLESTICKS have bobeche cups to catch melting wax. Handwork variances show in the arched bases. Plantation.

Tin PARADE or CAMPAIGN TORCHES swung on long or short poles, the Torches sometimes simply hooked over nails driven into fairly straight natural branches, popular during the period after 1850. The top unscrewed for filling and inserting a cotton waste wick that flared with a bright dependable flame. The unpleasant odor of its kerosene was ignored outdoors in the pandemonium of torchlight processions and spirited political rallies.

Brass CANDLESTICKS 1790-1820 have unusually thick glass chimneys, each fitted into a wide brass collar; (with a piece broken out the left is unsteady). Round lower holes permit air into the glass accelerating the brightness of the flames for better light and decreasing the heat and sooty smoke deposits on the insides of the shades. Between is fragrant Lavender Cotton from the garden. Plantation.

A mid-1800s childs' BATHING TUB with tinner-wrapped seams, applied carrying handles, and soapstained traces of inside white was red on the outside, one of the favorite early colors for tinware. Plantation.

During the mid to latter 1800s this heavy shiny white porcelain FOOTBATH with applied underglaze handles was said by its present owners to have been used nightly as a footbath; soothing to earlier prairie menfolks who had been working all day in the fields. (Abercrombie).

Replacing a Battlin' or Pounding Stick is this handcut wooden WASHBOARD. Its top corrugations, cut sharper and narrower for less soiled clothes, show little wear. Below the divider space the wider and more roundly cut ridges are white from soap lyes and worn from years of contact with dirtier garments; this chore ever a source of tired backs and enlarged and rough reddened knuckles for the early homemaker. 1800s.

A step from the corrugated scrubbing a wooden factory stamped HOME WASHER Pat. dated May 21, 1882, WRINGER has an iron handle, gears, and enclosed adjusting side springs. Patterned after a smooth Wringer the large corrugated roller caught and revolved the small rollers beneath, mangling and squeezing out wet clothes run through. Iron-clamped to a tub it was a contraption any Settler's wife would have had a fit over.

From the 1700s a pine TRENCHER (for carving and/or serving food) was fashioned from a single block of wood. About 15" in diameter it dwarfs the primitively-handsome charm of the double salt cups on a center handle, this too carved from one piece of pine in the same early century. (Abercrombie).

The smallest oak CHURN at left has an iron lifting and hanging ring while its top is handcut with a convenient gripknob. Its dasher handle is pulled up to show how wear against the center hole of the lid has worn it thin and corrugated.

The right hickory CHURN has a separate splash top that lifts off when the dasher is raised. Each of these Churns has wide discolored brass bands; 1860s.

Earlier handcrafted, 1830-1840, the large cedar CHURN is more unusual. Its square lid also fits down into the Churn (but farther into the recessed top) to prevent the cream splattering out during churning but this dasher ROCKS back and forth as opposed to being dashed up and down. An oblong hole cut at center restricts the Dasher from hitting the sides of the container. The irregularly auger-bored holes permit the cream to slide easily through the paddle.

A Berks County, Pennsylvania collection of BUTTER STAMPS c: 1860-1890 are in varied shapes and sizes; hollow-cut patterns of Dutch Tulips, Pinwheels, Flowers, Hearts, Ferns, and Pineapples that impressed raised designs called "prints" on pound (or larger) pats of butter. (Abercrombie).

When she'd dug it all uv taters frum th' patch with th' smithy-made DIGGIN FORK th' woman laid off th' apern she'd sewed t' warsh up afore supper, usin' th' WARSHRAG 'n TOWEL torn from meal sacks and LYE SOAP in the ironstone SOAP DISH. All were kept at th' warshtrough or on a plank table outside the back door, but indoors in bad weather. Here too was a wooden bucket of cool well water with a tinner-made "ev'rybody's cup" dangling over the edge to slake a thirst . . . or pour water over a sunbaked head. Beneath was another bucket of spare warshwater ready t' fill a handy warshbasin. Used water was tossed on vines and flowers planted closeby, nothing wasted.

The maple handcut Pennsylvania Dutch BOOTJACK has wood pegs extending through holding a block below to briefly tip one end. Placing the right bootclad foot on the solid end, the left heel could be hooked against the open edge and pulled to force off the stiff leather. In reverse the right boot could be removed.

A Dutch tulip is cut at the top right prong. Placed "right under his nose at th' door" hopefully th' mister would leave off his mudcaked field clodhoppers. About 1860.

Below the Berks County Butter Stamps in the old pine OPEN CUPBOARD are various other BUTTER STAMPS and MOLDS, three on the last shelf with handles up. Between at the right of the 4-petal flower MOLD is a rare tiny wooden BUTTER & PASTRY ROLLER, a minute design for transfer, made by the Moravians at Waldboro, Maine, 1800-1830. These are flanked by a CUPBOARD from Connecticut 1840 in original red paint holding pewter and a very early natural finished Maine closed CUPBOARD of the same period. (Abercrombie).

A 1-board top Figured Maple SUGARCHEST is considered by some to be one of the purest and most sought after forms in wood and style for this furniture. It has a wide lower drawer and although the golden brass pulls are not the original, they are from a similar artifact of the same period. These Chests were habitually kept locked to remove temptation from avid appetites. 1850.

A solid walnut Pennsylvania Dutch COUNTRY CUPBOARD made c. 1840 is 50" x 7' tall with its original blown glass set in frames grooved to match the doors and the top 4" cornice, practical for storage below and display above. Random width boards right from the place finished inside only form the back; dovetailed drawers have well turned pulls extending inside as their own woodscrews; two latches are replacements. Each base side is gracefully reverse-curved while a 4" deep pie shelf has increased height behind its 2" dropped frame.

Such narrow spaces held lots of Shoo-fly (Molasses) and Schnitz (Dried Apple) Pies ready for cutting into quarters for eager appetites. Even today most German homes of the Dutch Counties observe one day a week as Baking Day, and in eastern Pennsylvania the acknowledged best bakers are always called on to supply innumerable Funeral (Raisin) Pies.

Country-made of walnut when other woods as poplar were more commonly used this 53" high KITCHEN (PIE) SAFE with is original brass key has 35" wide shelves for cooling and storing freshly baked tempters. Less skillful than framed in wood, these punched-out ventilating panels nailed inside are much improved over those nailed on the outside, each tin here stamped "Pat. Dec. 21, 1883". The 15" high legs didn't totally protect for gnaw marks reveal some 4-legged intruders were intent on feasts of their own.

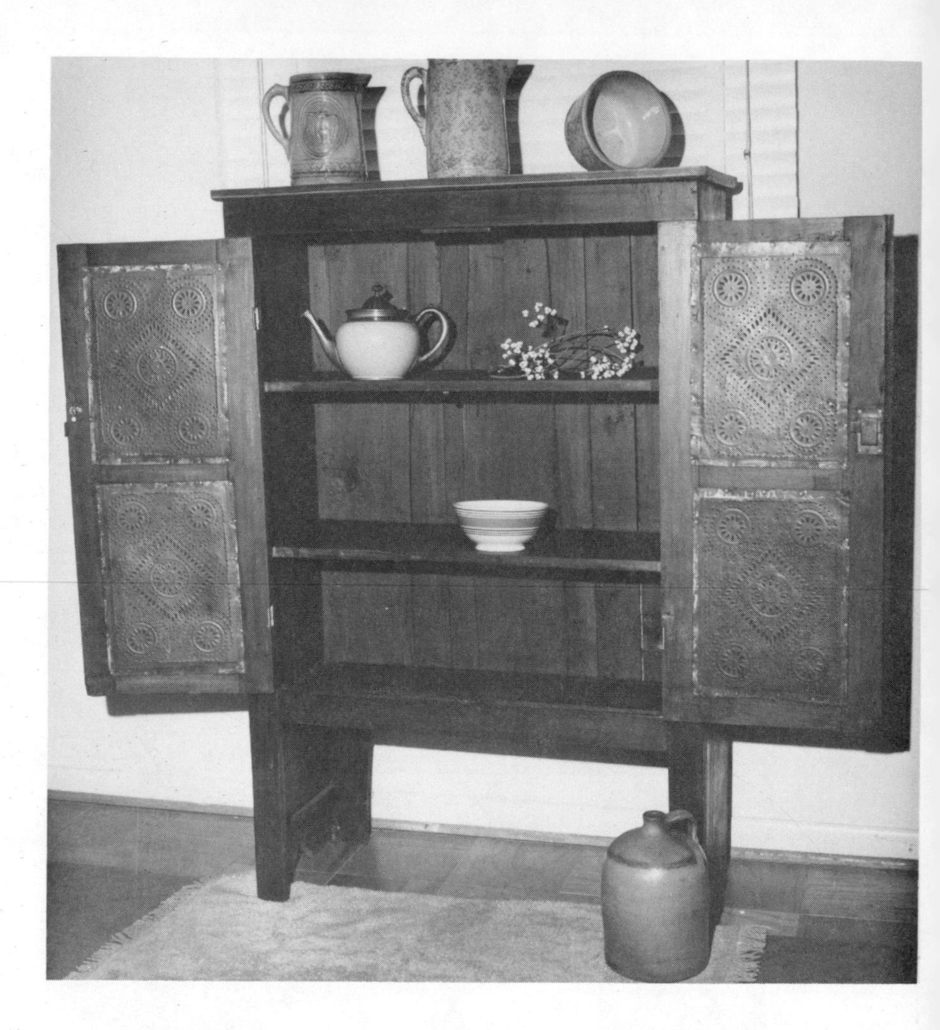

A fully-glazed stoneware PITCHER at left top has softly green cow medallions; the MILK PITCHERS, rarely seen blue on blue "Paw Print", one of the earliest sponge-daubing designs; slightly irregular in shape there are still none of the flakes and cracks so often found in such sensitive old softwares.

Th' Missus really DID Sharpen her knives on the edge of this CALICO SALTCROCK. Rather than put it off "till th' Mister found time t'git at hit", if she found a knife dull when she "wuz a fixin' t' use it" she simply whacked a good honing herself.

From the 1800s like these others, is an azure blue GRANITE TYPE (very fine) and PEWTER TEAPOT. The blue striped white CLABBER BOWL handed down from a'ways back had been tenderly wrapped in a shawl and carried onto a raw landgrant homestead where it looked "nice" on a rough plank table . . . and brought "back home" a little closer.

Departing from customarily simple lines this handcrafted KITCHEN (PIE) SAFE has intricately punched star design tins set in frames, the most expert method. Sap has caused the right center door panel to lighten, which is often typical of cherrywood. The knobs are replaced to the original. 1830.

A pine breadboard top TABLE 1830 has a wide apron and hardwood legs. Four Hitchcock type SIDE CHAIRS c: 1840 are maple with the plank pine seats cut wider at the backs; front legs are turned with wider-splayed rear straight legs.

A pewter CHARGER and two large pewter SPOONS (and an apple) are on the Table with a small brass TAVERN LAMP having a fingerhold. 1850. Abercrombie.

An Innkeeper gave one of these small Lamps to each guest with just enough oil to see him safely into bed after an evening of good food and fellowship; thus making certain if the Lamp spilled there would be no damage since the wick was only briefly saturated.

A similar size Lamp contained just a little more oil, called a COURTING LAMP. A young lady's father lit it when her young man came to call "of an evening". When the oil had burned down it was time for the "steady" to leave.

Hammered and shaped from hot iron two of the blades of these last-century CHOPPING KNIVES are single tang. At left the double tang extends through the handle and is folded over for strength. They were among the busiest of the early pantry tools because food had to be preserved. In preparation these Knives chopped meats, vegetables, fruits . . . all sorts of victuals to proper size. Held sideways the round-base cutters scraped every particle from the wooden chopping bowls, leaving a network of tiny crisscross lines. Fast disappearing by the early 1900s these Knives are now being eagerly sought for display and use.

A rarely-perfect SPONGEWARE PITCHER with blue daubs on a white background has a deeper wide blue band and partial inside pattern; the natural color EGG CROCK has narrow blue bands, a shiny glaze and a wire bail (handle). Both from the 1800s.

Maker-signed the right red clay JUG has an appealingly crooked shape, applied handle, and partial inside and outside deep brown glaze. The droplet mark appears on other such Jugs, some not signed, probably in itself one potter's touchmark.

The center white JUG with wooden top and restored iron bail (handle) held homegrown cucumbers cured into pickles.

The left fully glazed JUG for storing vinegar originally had a wooden plug top.

These stoneware artifacts made during the 1800s were non-porous and thus invaluable in storing molasses, cider, preserves and the like. All were found at Social Circle, Georgia.

As the story goes, homesteaders in that area used to regularly gather at a centrally located spring to barter among themselves and with nearby friendly Indians. As they swapped gossip, drank the cooling waters, and rested up for the trip back home everyone was so sociable the name of Social Circle just sort of happened . . . and it remains today.

All country artifacts of the latter 1800s include a blue on gray SALT CROCK with original LID, an inside curved stoneware open SALT CROCK with an Indian Head faintly left on one side, a bailed EGG CROCK, and a SPONGEWARE BOWL advertising an Iowa Mercantile Store (which might have been given as the customer paid his book account as was the custom so often in the "good old days".)

A wooden all-purpose LIDDED BOX with a Pennsylvania Dutch patterned Lid in its original paint c: 1870 could have been used for spices, biscuits, yarns . . . all manner of things as it was needed. (Abercrombie).

A sliding weight brass STEELYARD (Stilyerds) SCALE has an iron pan, these in use since fifteenth century England. A much later SHREDDER on the wall has at left below a dovetailed wooden SALT BOX, a LIDDED PAN for baking brown bread, and stoneware JUGS. Among the earliest this big nail pierced hammered sheet-tin FOOD GRATER is held to its handcut board with square nails. Such size making the work go faster it was constantly used to grate potatoes for yeast and starch and carrots for an extract to color pale butter. (This latter was especially true in winter when cows were not on green pasture.) Early to mid-1800s . . . Plantation.

On a random width planked floor are a cherry DOUGH RAISER, a LIGHT and a HEAVY DOUGH ROLLER (the latter with bored holes filled with tiny lead show and the holes leadpegged to flatten "Heavy" Dough).

12-stick CANDLE MOLD. Plantation early to mid 1800s.

On A fieldstone hearth worn smooth a rare earthenware COFFEE POT with tinner's bands kept brew fairly warm on its high wrought IRON TRIVET at the rim of cooling coals.

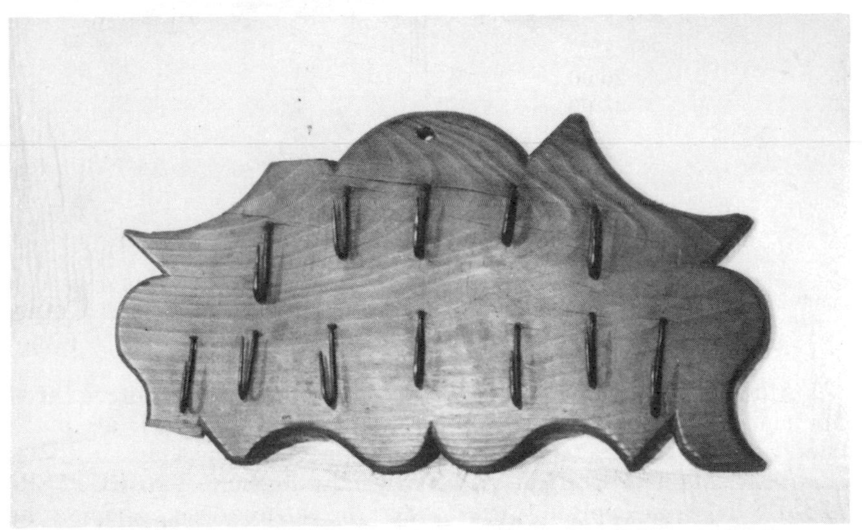

From 1700s Pennsylvania with only two corners broken in so long this walnut PANTRY BOARD held utensils on a wall convenient to open hearth cooking. Likely a weddin' presunt, after he or the local carpenter cut the board, the smithy made small holes with a Burn Auger, then forged slim iron hooks which he inserted and bent down on the back about an inch. An excellent example of handsomeness in a primitive.

All of this TREENWARE (the ancient plural of trees) save three are maple. The rarely small BUTTERWORKING BOWL at top is cherry with a base drainage hole later woodpegged. The short BISCUIT ROLLER retains a whiff of its cedarwood pungency. Two BUTTER-MOLDS have pineapple patterns (one of the earliest designs popular in New England) while the other with a wildflower stamp came from Bledsoe's Lick, Tennessee (settled in 1779 and the scene of an Indian Massacre). No mistaking the feel and wearmarks on these old BUT-TERSCRAPERS. Held upside down the Paddle restrained the butter as the nick permitted liquids to drain out.

A 1700s carver looked long and hard to find the proper beechwood for this large DOUGH TRAY. Almost exactly grained at either end (one pierced for hanging) an original center unevenness is accentuated by paddle and spoon scraping. Equally old is this STIRRIN' an' TASTIN' SPOON . . . its handcut solid piece of maple strength having agitated endless cornmeal mush and puddin's.

An 1800s 1-piece handcut off-center-handle FOODSTOMPER and DOUGHROLLER with two skillfully wrought iron DOUGHBOARD SCRAPERS. A later COOKIE CUTTER recalls the big ginger and molasses treats Grandmas baked for several centuries . . . as the children balanced goodies in both hands she said if they dropped a cookie it would mash their toes. The SUGAR SCOOP is one piece of handlapped tin with an applied handle.

Whole peach-shaped nutmegs brought from the East Indies and stored in the top lidded section of this tin NUTMEG GRATER Sifted out at the open bottom when grated on the tool's rounded pierced side. Mace the shell was not wasted, its flavor somewhat heavier.

Miniature graters were regularly carried in purses and weskits to spice beverages (at home and in taverns) and improve at table the flavor of occasional bland foods.

Many who publicly loudly scorned using tobacco, behind locked doors finely-grated the hardpressed dried plugs on these same small graters into powdered snuff . . . and sniffed . . . secretly.

This habit . . . tobacco that could be inhaled . . . peaked in the 1700s but was no longer fashionable after about 1830.

A low WAGONCHAIR with shorter rear legs "so's a'body wunt pitch outa th' cheer on ther haid" in a wagonbed lumbering along over cart trails and corduroy roads (logs laid crossways side by side) where rocks and slip'ry mudholes were the rule. An extra seat when the large families had "vis'tin kin on their hearth", it carried them "t'weddin's, buryin's, quiltin's, cabin-raisin's, preachin's, 'n huskin' bees". When not in use it hung on a wooden peg driven into the wall near the low ceiling. c: 1850. Plantation.

Note the TRAMMEL HOOK on a swinging CRANE, copper COOKING PANS, wall COFFEE GRINDER, small SAUSAGE STUFFER, lidded SPIDER for baking in hardwood coals raked out onto the hearth, iron KETTLE, strings of RED PEPPERS, and LADLES, SKIMMERS, and TESTERS. 1850.

At the Plantation the Cook presently in charge uses these same utensils from an earlier day to exhibit (for the pleasure of tourists) delicious cornpone, bread dressing, and sweet potato pies in the Lidded Spiders set in the coals, no small feat without burning.

Fancier than most from the 1845 or any period this beautifully-grained pine WOODBOX has surprisingly large cannonball finials turned on a foot treadle lathe. Plantation.

The oblong DOUGHBOWL was often placed upside down on left-over biscuits, pone, etc. on the table or pantry shelf as a deterrent to insects and even larger critters. However, the latter's efforts were determined and made the "gnawed dint." One end is pierced for wall hanging. The round cherry MIXING BOWL with the nicely-grooved rim was made for a bride about 1870. The left ROLLER by far the older of the two doubled as a FOOD STOMPER while its companion DOUGH ROLLER still has traces of flour deep in its cracks.

These pantry tools have continued in usage for many generations.

A maple LITTLE BOSTON ROCKING CHAIR c: 1850, smaller than the regular Boston Rocker, also termed a sewing or nursing chair, in this case stood at the kitchen hearth. The wide seat is slightly rolled, there are five back spindles, the legs are socketed into the rockers. (The earliest Rockers were the same distance out front fron the two legs as they extended at the back from the rear two legs.) Plantation.

Rocking where the whole family begged hot Benne Seed cakes it must have crushed countless dropped crumbs. (Benne Seed was well liked in baking, Benne a plant carried from West Africa to our Carolina coastal regions, said to bring good luck to those who garden planted or ate of it.)

Rockers, deemed by most as wholly American, have an indistinct history, mentioned as appearing briefly in Europe far into the 1600s. But they did evolve here probably during the early 1700s and it is recorded that around 1762 Eliakim Smith, a Massachusetts cabinet-maker, was kept busy putting them on cottage (straight) chairs. By 1810 American Rocking Chairs were becoming established, the Boston type ever most popular . . . ever called "the Boston" no matter in which part of our country it was made.

WINDSOR TYPE COMBBACK ROCKING CHAIR c: mid-1800s is maple with a wide pine seat. American Windsors deviated from their English origins with an airier light appearance, being easier to pick up and move about. It has a good wide leg splay, the greater the angling the better for sturdiness. After 1725 American Windsors had "arrived" and continued most popularly through the 1800s. (Abercrombie).

A cherry PLANTATION (secretary) DESK handfashioned c: 1850 in North Carolina is almost 7' tall. Below the 5" cornice and upper doors is a 1" carved beading, half as wide around the original blown glass doors, each carved section showing distinctive touches of several place-trained woodworkers, always obvious in individual crafting even though each participant follows the same pattern. A 21" door drops open as a writing surface and behind that are shelves, pigeonholes, dividers for tall record books of people and plantation operation, and a few dried seed grains spilled from small cloth bags once held for test plantings. The whole top section lifts off, held to the base openback table by its own weight with two large wooden pegs fitting into slots. Lightly smoothed random width boards form the Desk's back and the long shallow dovetailed drawer has wooden knobs that self-fasten inside as turnings; spool legs are only 36" high; each section can be separately locked with original brass keys.

For other than immediate needs later frontier dwellers cut and held to air-dry their native woods as apple, walnut, pine, cedar, poplar, chestnut, cypress, sycamore, etc. awaiting the arrival of an itinerant cabinetmaker in his wagon; or, as they grew more affluent, trained their own field hands showing desires or natural aptitudes to be expert craftsmen. (Objects inside for background display.)

A rare NURSING CHAIR whose high back and wide seat are close-woven basketweave. The original painted design is only faint now on the headrest; bowed-out arms extend only halfseat; the legs are set into the rockers; and baby could be laid across the lap and rocked without its bumping either side of the Chair.

In the background is a large COPPER APPLEBUTTER KETTLE, a small legged castiron POT for soups and stews, and a griddle. 1848-1850. Plantation.

Found in Massachusetts this MAIDEN carved from green oak is thought to have been the guardian on a vessel sailing out of New Bedford in the early 1800s, steadfastly watching from her niche on a sheltered deck panel high above the stern.

Surpassing in beauty the inevitable harshness of the Settlers' basic primitives she still relates through an individual's desire to fashion something fine with his own hands . . . but in a more relaxed circumstance in the same era.

The weathered nose only enhances her appeal, natural carving variances are in her expressive eyes, the dimple in her chin, the flowers in her hair. She may have painstakingly emerged under the knives of the ship's carpenter during a voyage to the South Seas; an American Indian Maiden native to that New England coast could have been reflected.

But no matter . . . whoever . . . and wherever the inspiration of her beginnings . . . she remains today as yours to imagine.

During the city's rebuilding after its disastrous Chicago Fire in 1871 building facades, especially along the Gold Coast, were embellished with a wide assortment of cherubs, warriors, urns, and so on. Found in an abandoned southside warehouse this handsome SHIELD is one of those molds seldom seen or recognized today . . . a ZINC STAMPING into which a durable type plaster was poured to harden in forming one of these decorations.

ON BUYING

Once upon a hundred years ago a man himself owning vast acreage steadily advised: "Buy all the land you can, there will never be any more". The same "nevermore" exists among originals from our American beginnings.

It is physically impossible to successfully reproduce feel and wear-marks on glass, for instance, and the patina of old woods. However, if copies or similars are of good quality and workmanship and if YOU are satisfied . . . enjoy them; they might even be tomorrow's collectibles. But that which is junk now will not be improved by a thousand years' growth . . . if it should last that long!

Many factors are to be considered in buying; current pricing is subject to age, condition, signatures and touchmarks, rarity, originality of design, finish, skillful repairs, the economics of an area, and the immediate popular trend of a locale's collector-interest. Prices at good professional sources are generally fair but with today's professional costs new items, particularly glass and porcelains, could be more expensive than the original and not nearly so well made. It is a personal choice.

Some folks took better care of their belongings than others; overall some wear is inevitable and even desirable, but if rust and exposure have too deeply pitted iron or dryrot is present in wood, better to avoid such pieces . . . a few wormholes compliment. Those seeking home furniture should check for practical strength and suitable size, skillful repairs being no deterrent (except if the object is museum bound where they prefer their own decisions and craftsmen).

Softwears in pottery were suspectible to chips and cracks. Minor chips are mildly acceptable but there is customer resistance to cracks (spiders) that will leak in usage or if there is intent to sell or trade later. A marriage, most often in furniture, being parts from several related old pieces combined to form one good piece may be just fine if honestly presented . . . it could be even more durable and attractive than if allowed to remain for sale ugly and rickety.

Reputable dealers sell only what they would be willing to buy for themselves. If a poor item appears in a box of goodies they will sell the first marked "as is" and priced accordingly; these make adequate cabinet pieces.

Antique browsing/buying can be an engrossing activity for family togetherness; I recall a 12-year-old who became interested in Civil War Artifacts as his mother delighted in art glass and his father was absorbed in clocks. Many younguns and teens are collecting early comic books, coins, and stamps; even tourists are spotting and securing old limestone fenceposts which midwestern quarries produced in the days of the first barbed wire strung on the prairies and our far-western ranches.

To become more comfortable and knowledgeable in buying and recognition, visit as many shops, libraries, shows and seminars, fleamarkets, garage sales of known good old pieces, art exhibits, and auctions as possible. Look good . . . listen good . . . and ask questions. Read every book you can on the subject best suited to your interests and then enlarge your field to other categories for general information and entertainment. We are what we see . . . how we judge what we hear . . . what we read . . . and our personal application of all these.

At auctions a piece seen beforehand as perfect or nearly so might have later received a noticeable imperfection from many handlings. Examine everything, particularly the perishables, as soon as you have obtained the bid; if damage was skipped over or if the piece is not as presented by the caller, return it immediately to the cashier's desk, to be relayed to those in charge. (To wait is to risk not being able to return it later.) Customarily rules are given before bidding begins; if such are not announced, stand up and find out what they are before participating. Understand, also, exactly what your bid covers. (My nephew once successfully bid on a "box" of whatevers. Ready to leave he proceeded to pay his chit, only then becoming aware that for his price he had bought a "roomful" of boxed miscellanies).

The auctioneer is only human and he too makes mistakes in putting hundreds of items across the podium in a limited time. Thus, better not wave to a friend, pull at your nose, scratch your head, nod in answer to a companion . . . you might have something you don't want and never intended bidding. Be alert when you are bidding, passive when you are not.

Dealers seldom bid beyond their own evaluation of a realistic price for resale (unless a customer has otherwise instructed them). Collectors bid to the extent of their purses and desires . . . not always in that order. Many of yesterday's necessities are among today's luxuries. So buy what YOU like and will be willing to have around the house for awhile. Should you later change your mind there are always professionals who will be pleased to sell on consignment at your mutually agreed price, the dealer charging a currently accepted percentage of the sale.

(Only Plantation artifacts are not priced, these herein for your enjoyment through courtesy-interest of the museum restoration; to afford an even better understanding of how intensely such additional pieces portray the tremendous individual scope of our historical Primitives. However, there are "similars" or "related kin" given so you might average out accordingly.)

Prices given are GUIDES . . . to point the buyer in the right direction . . . a REPORT of actual price tags fastened to each item purchased or noted for sale, principally with licensed outlets.

Prices here are meant, also, to aid in determining the MEASURE of VALUE . . . from these prices how the items are being now regarded as to their RANGE of worth. The difference between present commodities and antiques is that while commodities go up or down antiques only go up, slowly but surely. Quality antiques have for the past several years been deemed good investments by authoritative financial sources. At a 1978 auction a rare handwoven signed and dated coverlet went to a private collector bidding over $5000, this far beyond the pre-sale advertising estimate of $1500 maximum; just one example confirming the belief of many that there is no "top dollar" in any category for its best antiques, not many primrose paths left with Pandora's Boxes at the ends waiting with discovery bargains. However, the exception usually proves a rule so occasionally there are sleepers and anyone can get lucky.

Prices for Primitives cannot be achieved as can those items where artists produced a definite style in a known period. Primitives encompass infinite variations . . . they are timeless . . . prices almost so in scale . . . as individual as the Primitives themselves.

For all these reasons I would not presume to set an exact immediate cost on every piece "like or similar to" what I have shown, but these do establish the nucleus from which one can operate . . . thus . . .

Spend carefully . . . if you like antiques and collectibles, buy and use or just-plain-enjoy-them-to-look-at . . . once exposed few can resist . . . AND

While antiquing one meets the nicest people!

INDEX AND PRICES

Item	Page	Price
Cabinet, Pennsylvania Dutch	154	1200.00 up
Calipers	136,137	26.00- 50.00
Candleholder, iron	82	48.00
mold, 12-tube*	162	
similar		110.00-125.00 up
Candlestick, bobeche cup*	146	
brass*	147	
similars		175.00-250.00 pair
single brass	94	95.00
wooden double*	145	
similar		175.00-195.00
Canteen, burnished iron, large	107	100.00-175.00
Carriage, fifth wheel	51	40.00
steps	119	25.00
Carving	173	300.00-375.00
Chair, child's*	70	
similar		28.00
Hitchcock type	157	625.00 set of 4
wagon*	167	
similar		75.00- 95.00
Chamberstick, pushup	140	95.00-125.00
Chant	29	
Cheese, basket	83	295.00-300.00
ford	84	75.00-95.00
ditch	84	425.00
Church pew, primitive	141	165.00-195.00 up
"ca." for circa	10	
Clapboards	45	
Clinchcutter	126	18.00
Coalsaver	131	22.50- 25.00
Coffeegrinder, wall*, similar	167	45.00- 65.00
lap	143	50.00 variable
pot, earthenware*	163	
similar		150.00-175.00
tinned with copper	79	95.00-115.00
Commander	18	50.00
clevis type	126	5.00
tool	60	45.00
Cookie cutter	166	10.00
Cooper's Chamfering knife	135	110.00-115.00
gouge	135	35.00
hoopsetter	135	45.00-50.00
sawtooth	135	45.00- 50.00

Item	Page	Price
Copper Pitcher & Bowl	74	175.00-195.00
Cornsheller, hand	59	19.00-22.50
Cotton gin	30	35.00
Coverlet, 1840	142	300.00-500.00 variable
1857	142	300.00-500.00 variable
Cracklin's squeezer	67	19.00
Cradle*	74	
similar		185.00
Crane, iron fireplace*	167	
similar		95.00 variable
Cresset	76	275.00
Crock, calico spongeware	156,160	95.00-125.00
egg, with bail	158,160	175.00-185.00
imprinted, 1 gallon	143	110.00 up
Indian head stamp	160	50.00
large lidded	87	50.00- 65.00
salt, lidded	160	100.00-115.00
sealing wax	87	35.00- 45.00 variable
storage		45.00- 55.00 variable
Cup, tinnermade	72	42.00
Cupboard, closed natural finish	153	1200.00 up
open, doors below	153	250.00-400.00
painted	153	1300.00-1800.00 up
primitive*	70	
(note prices for similar on others here)		
Curry comb	121	10.00
Dahlonega	39	
Desk, plantation secretary type	170,171	2200.00 variable
Dippers, tin	81	22.00- 28.00
Dividers	136	12.50- 18.00
Document carrier, tinnermade	11	95.00-100.00
Doorhasp	131	155.00
Doughboard scraper	166	35.00- 55.00
Dough bowl	168	135.00 up
mixing, wooden	168	125.00 up
cutter	80	95.00
raiser* see bowl above	162	
roller* see maple below	162	
maple	166,168	50.00 up
stomper	166,168	35.00
tray, large	143,165	175.00-225.00
Drawknife	134,135	40.00 variable
Dresser	143	450.00 variable
Dutch crown	103	175.00

Item	Page	Price
Sugar, chest	153	950.00 up
cleaver, nipper	22	250.00 up
maple mold, wooden carved	26	275.00
scoop, tin	166	12.50
skimmer, copper	22	75.00
Sunbonnet (old handmade)	92	35.00-45.00
Table, breadboard top	157	850.00 up
tavern	112	900.00 up
Tackle block	59	50.00
Tap, male	133	20.00
Tea caddy	112	115.00
jar	113	125.00
pot	156	150.00
Tobacco, counter cutter	38	45.00- 75.00
hiller	36	45.00
marker	37	45.00
peg	37	3.00-22.00 up
plants curing*	36	
plug and tag	37	6.00
shed*	36	
shipping box, printed	38	35.00
slicer	37	15.00 up
To growing towns	97	
Tongs, buggybrace	118	25.00
fire	118	25.00
hoop	124	22.50
log, railroad	117	45.00
smoking (ember)	118	75.00
special purpose	124	20.00
straight lip	124	20.00
Tool carrier	138	145.00 varies
Torch, parade or campaign	147	42.50
Touchmark, broadaxe	46	400.00-425.00
jug	159	25.00- 35.00 up
Trammel, adjustable straight edge	86,167*	125.00
chain type	78	195.00-295.00
long bars - also used as barrel lifts	78	110.00
sawtooth	83	195.00
Trap, bear	32	195.00 up
leghold small animal	31	35.00- 50.00
fox	31	85.00
Treenware	164	items individually priced

Item	Page	Price
Trencher, wooden, large	150	295.00
Trivet*	163	
similar		40.00 up
adjustable long iron	79	165.00
Trunk, wooden	115	165.00 varies
dome top	142	75.00 up
Tub, bathing*	148	
similar metal		145.00
foot	148	225.00
small wooden	85	50.00
Turpentine, adz	32	45.00 up
ladle	34	30.00 varies
scraper	34	35.00
slasher	35	25.00
spade	34	35.00
Utensil board, handfashioned	163	200.00-225.00
Vise*, wooden	64	
similar		40.00
Wagon, bangboards	51	
hauling	51	225.00 up
hammer	55	25.00
jack	56	85.00
joiner spike	55	20.00
stretcher	52	45.00
wheel, light wagon (in good condition)	50	45.00
Wall grouping	143	individually priced
Washboard	149	50.00 varies
Wash kettle, iron	92	75.00 varies
stick	92	22.00
tub	91,143	95.00
Wedge, iron	17	2.50
Well, bucket*	13	
similar, metal	13	25.00
long tube	16	35.00
windlass (wheel)	13,14	35.00
Whetstone carrier	27	125.00 each
Windmill weight, chicken	15	500.00-750.00 (more for original colors)
Woodbox*	168	
similar, pine		225.00
Wool carders	96	25.00- 40.00 pair
Wringer, wooden	150	50.00

*Stone Mountain Ante Bellum Plantation artifacts

The current values in this book should be used only as a guide. They are not intended to set prices, which vary from one section of the country to another. Auction prices as well as dealer prices vary greatly and are affected by condition as well as demand. Neither the Author nor the Publisher assumes responsibility for any losses that might be incurred as a result of consulting this guide.

Schroeder's Antiques Price Guide

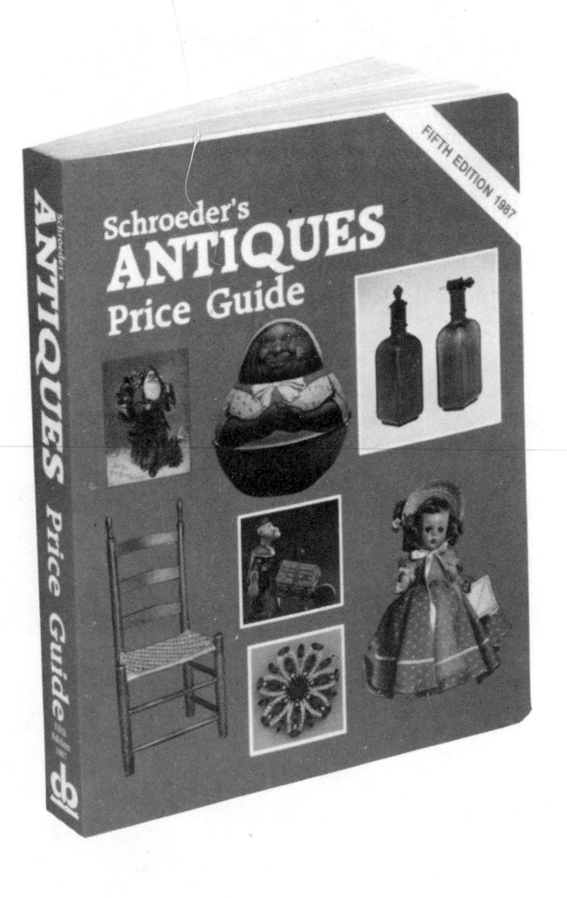

Schroeder's Antique *Price Guide* has climbed it way to the top in a fiel already supplied with severa well-established publication The word is out, *Schroeder Price Guide* is the best bu at any price. Over 50 categories are covered, wit more than 50,000 listing But it's not volume alone tha makes Schroeder's the un que guide it is recognized t be. From ABC Plates t Zsolnay, if it merits the in terest of today's collecto you'll find it in Schroeder's Each subject is represente with histories an background information. I addition, hundreds of shar original photos are used eac year to illustrate not only th rare and the unusual, but th everyday "fun-type" collec tibles as well -- not postag stamp pictures, but larg close-up shots that show im portant details clearly.

Each edition is completely re-typeset from all new sources. We have not and will no simply change prices in each new edition. All new copy and all new illustrations mak Schroeder's THE price guide on antiques and collectibles.

The writing and researching team behind this giant is proportionately large. It is backe by a staff of more than seventy of Collector Books' finest authors, as well as a board o advisors made up of well-known antique authorities and the country's top dealers, al specialists in their fields. Accurancy is their primary aim. Prices are gathered over the en tire year previous to publication, from ads and personal contacts. Then each category i thoroughly checked to spot inconsistencies, listings that may not be entirely reflective o actual market dealings, and lines too vague to be of merit. Only the best of the lot remain for publication. You'll find *Schroeder's Antiques Price Guide* the one to buy for factua information and quality.

No dealer, collector or investor can afford not to own this book. It is available from you favorite bookseller or antiques dealer at the low price of $11.95. If you are unable to fin this price guide in your area, it's available from Collector Books, P. O. Box 3009, Paducah KY 42001 at $11.95 plus $1.00 for postage and handling.